what others :

superplan: a journey into God's story recounts the fascinating missionary experiences of Chris Clayman. Each chapter uses a biblical passage and a personal encounter to show how God has provided fresh guidance to join Him on the front lines of Christian mission among the least-reached people of the earth. Of particular interest is the surprising insight of new believers into God's character and mission. Anyone who seeks to follow God's call to missions will be encouraged by this book.

George T. Russ
Executive Director, Metropolitan New York Baptist Association

From Texas to Mali to New York City, Chris does an excellent job of sharing his journey discovering and living out God's Superplan, including all of the honest and raw mountain tops and valleys that come with passionately pursuing the Lord. Clayman, as well as the friends and disciples he has made along the way, are true modern-day examples of people who have died to their own dreams and desires in order to follow Christ into the great unknown. May you be inspired as you submit to God's Superplan—starting in Jerusalem and going to the ends of the earth just as the Global Gates crew is doing.

Grant Haynes
Executive Director, Global Frontier Missions

Walk 100,000 miles in Chris's shoes as he discovers God's Superplan to redeem people from all the "ethne" of the earth. You may find the world shrink as you discover whom God has placed in your neighborhood. May the Body of Christ embrace the staggering opportunities of our day.

Sue Patt
Program Director, *Perspectives* Study Program

God is divinely orchestrating global migration and thereby opening the doors to reach people groups that have previously been difficult to reach. Chris's story is a wonderful example of how God moves in our lives to reach the nations that he brings to us. *Superplan* is a motivating read that encourages all believers into God's ultimate plan to reach the nations.

Kevin King
President, International Project, NYC

Chris is an authentically gentle and passionate soul who has gifted the Church with an epic travelogue spanning years and continents and chronicling discoveries of the highest possible significance. As you journey along in these pages, you will have the opportunity to discover yourself anew in the current of God's Superplan and his ever-advancing Kingdom.

Cody Lorance
President and CEO, Borderless

A new narrative for modern missions is emerging today as God leverages global cities to gravitate *ethne* for redemption. Geopolitical and religious hostility towards the gospel may have minimized the role of western missionaries in the foreign field, but by no means has it relieved them of their responsibility for missions. This book is a testament to the shift that we are seeing in missions, where God has not finished with us, and it gives hope to many who cannot travel overseas to do missions. With the stroke of his own life story, Chris paints a much-needed image of God's faithfulness and triumph over our seemingly unfortunate circumstances that can throw us off and even cast doubts as to our missionary call and worth.

Dr. Alfonse Javed
Missions Pastor at Calvary Baptist Church, NYC

Chris has made an incredible story deeply relatable and accessible, while at the same time inspiring us to greater obedience as global Christians. I was personally both humbled and challenged to hear afresh the voice of the Spirit in my own life and ministry. I would highly recommend this book to any who wish to immerse themselves in God's 'superplan' to reach the nations for Christ.

Valerie Althouse
NYC Area Director; International Students, Inc.
Founder/Director, English Connections Network

Chris Clayman has a remarkable heart for God. As I have worked with Chris, I have never seen a missionary more intentional about the use of his time to reach people who have not been reached. It was my privilege to be a part of his early days in New York City. His journey makes one realize what a great God we serve. It is stunning to see how God has taken his life and his wife Nichole's life and blessed so many.

Taylor Field
Pastor/Director Graffiti Church, New York City

As a former missionary to West Africa and current leader of a Great Commission organization, I have always appreciated Chris's authentic, heartfelt, and missiologically sound approach to reaching the unreached ... wherever they live! Paul said, "Follow me as I follow Christ." One would do well to follow Chris Clayman's example of a faithful follower, as it will inevitably lead to a life fully-dedicated to Christ's global purpose and glory.

Dr. David Pope
Executive Director, Issachar Initiative

superplan

superplan

a journey into God's story

chris clayman

WIGTake Resources

P.O. Box 1884, Monument, CO 80132

www.WIGTakeResources.org

Product Distribution: NoHutch@wigtake.org

ISBN:978-1-939124-14-2

1. Missions. 2. Evangelism.

Clayman, Chris 1978 –

Printed by Bookmasters

Cover Design by Mike Mirabella

Interior Design by Megan Chadwick

Websites: www.theSuperPlan.com

www.WIGTake.org

www.ChurchPlantingMovements.com/bookstore

www.GlobalGates.info

Clayman, Chris

        superplan, a journey into God's story

table of contents

For Nichole and our children

The names of some individuals and places in *Superplan* have been altered or excluded to protect their privacy, and in some cases, their security. Unless otherwise noted, all Scripture references are from the English Standard Version. All royalties from this book will support the ministries of Global Gates.

foreword

I first met Chris Clayman through his ethnographic survey of New York City, cleverly titled *ethNYcity: The Nations, Tongues, and Faiths of Metropolitan New York*. Shortly afterwards, I read Chris's missiological manifesto, "Reaching the Nations Through Our Cities" (2014, available at globalgates.info/resources), and told my wife, "This is the most compelling missiological article I've read in years!"

Before the year was over I found myself sitting on a bench in New York's Central Park listening to Chris share the remarkable story of how God led him from an ordinary life in a small Texas town on an extraordinary journey to the halls of Cambridge University, then into the Saharan villages beyond Timbuktu, before finally bringing his family to New York City.

In New York's Harlem and Bronx neighborhoods, Chris and his family have immersed themselves in communities of West African immigrants, and positioned themselves squarely within portals, global gateways, that have opened up gospel highways to the very ends of the earth.

The world has changed; no longer do immigrants burn their bridges behind them. Instead, they remain connected through phone, the internet, and intercontinental travel with the homelands from which they come. Simply put, this means when we reach them here, we reach them there! Chris has experienced this strategic connection through

Muslim-background Christians in New York who have opened doors for planting churches and making disciples in West Africa.

Today dozens of others have moved into global gateway cities across North America, joining Chris and Global Gates in reaching the ends of the earth through these strategic immigrant communities in our own back yard. As one missions minister put it, "For years we have been sending our very best to the ends of the earth. Today the ends of the earth are sending their very best to us!"

Superplan is the back story, Chris's personal story, behind this remarkable Great Commission breakthrough. I must confess that I, too, have been caught up in God's superplan that connects my life to God's extraordinary grace-filled plan for all mankind. As you read this book, it is my prayer that you, too, will be caught up in God's superplan for your life, and for the nations.

Dr. David Garrison
Executive Director, Global Gates

we are all just actors

1

O Lord, you have searched me and known me! You know when I sit down and when I rise up; you discern my thoughts from afar. You search out my path and my lying down and are acquainted with all my ways. Even before a word is on my tongue, behold, O Lord, you know it altogether. You hem me in, behind and before, and lay your hand upon me. Such knowledge is too wonderful for me; it is high; I cannot attain it (Psalm 139:1-6).

EVADING THE SCOURGE OF the West African sun, four village elders and I lounged under a mango tree in Bandogo, Mali. The mango trees' shade functioned as air conditioners in the village, and the elders and honored guests had the best spots reserved.

Once, on a canoe trip to Timbuktu, the fabled Saharan city in my adopted country of Mali, I measured the temperature at 138 degrees Fahrenheit in the sun and a cool 108 degrees in the shade. When the wind blew, heat blasted our faces like an opened oven door.

Despite the heat, Bandogo men covered most of their body with clothing. A typical outfit consisted of a *boubou* (matching pants and flowing robe that extend past the knees) and a *kufi* (a Muslim skull cap) or toboggan cap (the type worn by Westerners in colder weather than Malians can imagine).

Their caps offered some resistance to the sun, but the mango trees' shade made the "sun season"[1] bearable. One of the more comical events of village life occurred when the sun moved, and the old men shuffled chairs chasing the shifting shade. On this particular day, one of the four village elders commenced the shuffle game by grumbling, "The sun is large today." Then, grabbing the arms of his chair, he shuffled several feet to his right to catch the shade. The rest of us shuffled after him, and we picked up our conversation where we left off. We continued this game every 30 minutes or so; it was hard to tell. The sun's position was the village's only indication of time.

We endured "the period of the sun's peak" under the shade, sometimes talking, and sometimes silent or sleeping. We conversed about religion and politics, topics my American culture taught me to avoid. The people of Bandogo also loved talking about the United States. "Let me see those sandals," one elder demanded from me in the Bambara language.[2] I had bought the sandals for less than two dollars at Walmart—the cheapest shoes money could buy in America. "Ah, you see these shoes," the man exclaimed as he tugged on the rubber. "These shoes come from America." He continued in admiration, "Surely, they will last forever." I resisted telling him they were from China.

A week earlier, at the age of 23, I made the village of Bandogo my home. The mud-hut village lacked running water, electricity, postal service, telephones, cell service, paved roads, and shops. The closest weekly market was several miles away. I moved among the people of Bandogo because they belong to the Wassoulou people group; no one in my mission organization had heard of a Wassoulou church—or even a Wassoulou Christian living among the Wassoulou.[3]

For the first time in my life, I could fit all my belongings (a battery-operated lamp, a mosquito net, several outfits, and a few other items) in a single suitcase. To become the first follower of Jesus living in Bandogo, I emptied myself of possessions, conveniences, and my previous way of life, but an old man rewarded my efforts by tugging on China-made Walmart thong sandals in awe of my riches. I was upset and disturbed. "If only he knew," I thought to myself. But he was right. I was a rich man. And I became keenly aware of the few items I still possessed in my little mud hut.

We are All Just Actors

Over 15 years have passed since I left Bandogo, Mali. I live in New York City now, in the Bronx. I have a wife (Nichole), a son, and two daughters, and my family has never lived together in Africa.

I never knew my life could experience the depth of physical, emotional, and spiritual struggle induced by that African village—

and that my response to the struggle would change myself, that village, and countless others. I was also unaware of how seemingly unconnected people and places could be so intertwined. In my story: Abilene, Texas connects to Cambridge University; Cambridge connects to Japanese friends; Japanese friends connect to Mali, and Mali connects to Manhattan. All of these connections are part of God's story, and this book reveals how I (and others) became a part of his *Superplan*.

One afternoon in Manhattan, two blocks from where John Lennon was murdered outside his Dakota apartment building,[4] I sat on a bench with a Muslim immigrant from Senegal named Abou. We ate lamb gyros,[5] shooed pigeons from our bench, reminisced about Africa, and conversed about the story of the Bible. Abou said:

> *Reading through the Bible is amazing! It makes me see that God plans everything. Life is like a movie, and God is the director. The prophets—they are like the actors. Other people are extras. Satan is the bad guy. It is like we are all part of a movie. I find myself wondering, "What is the responsibility of humans now?"*

Abou relayed his thoughts on the Bible with a freshness and insight that come from someone who hasn't been inoculated with Bible stories since childhood—which often provides enough Bible familiarity to strip away the story's power but not enough faith and application to positively affect. Abou was reading the Bible for the first time, but he articulated a truth that took me many trials, and miracles, to discover. Our stories are, at best, subplots to a larger one. We are just actors—maybe even extras—in a grander story than our own.

When we become aware of the larger story we are in, we can rise above self-focused interpretations of our stories. We can also transcend the interpretations of others. There may be truth in those interpretations. There may not be. Ultimately, we must find truth and interpret our life by understanding its place within God's greater story.

"True character development," wrote theologian Kevin Vanhoozer, "is *theodramatic*: understanding oneself as caught up in God's play of making all things new in and through Christ."[6] Abou, my gyro-eating Muslim friend, simply says, "God is the director."[7]

In this book, I introduce a word to help the theme stick. A Bangladeshi friend named Aslam, whose story I will tell toward the end of the book, often says, "I have no need to worry, because I am a part of God's Superplan."

A Superplan! Sometimes it takes a non-native-English speaker to inject fresh meaning into our language. God's Superplan is the redemptive story of God, rooted in eternity, recorded in the Bible, and realized even today. God's Superplan transcends our strengths and weaknesses, victories and sufferings, ideas and efforts. In dramatic ways, God is drawing people into knowledge and love of him from all peoples and areas of the world. This redemptive story is one God does not keep to himself. Instead, he beckons us to leave our mundane, small plans to join him in his Grand Narrative.

None of us begin life in God's Superplan. We begin where we are, and may remain there until God draws us into something bigger, bigger even than the great state of Texas where my story began.

---

[1] There are two main seasons in Mali: rainy season and dry season. The dry season has a "cold season" in which the temperature is warm during the day but cool at night. It also has a "hot season" in which the temperature is scorching, and a cloud of dust hangs in the air from Sahara winds (called the *Harmattan*).

[2] Polite words like "please" or "may I" do not exist in Bambara. Outsiders think Malians are fighting when they talk! Words are choppy, and Malian faces seem to express anger while talking. Most of the time, however, they are joking. They act offended and retaliate with verbal barbs in jest. For instance, Malians call each other "slaves" or "bean eaters" based on the other's last name and lineage. Although these barbs sound condescending to the Western ear, Malians believe the joking relationships keep ethnic rivals at peace.

[3] One exception could be a village we heard of where a Catholic church exists, if Wassoulou were indeed among them. Later, we discovered a couple of isolated Christians in various villages.

[4] My office is located two blocks from the Dakota building. There is an "Imagine" mosaic next to the building in Central Park where Beatles-addicts pay homage to John Lennon. Yoko Ono still lives in the Dakota.

[5] *Halal* (Muslim-approved) gyro carts have replaced hot dog stands as kings of the NYC food-cart scene. One of my daughter's favorite foods is gyros. She often asks, "Daddy, may we please, please have *halal* today?" She's a New Yorker!

[6] Kevin Vanhoozer, *Faith Speaking Understanding: Performing the Drama of Doctrine* (Louisville: Westminster John Knox Press, 2014), 131.

[7] While I outlined this book, I came across an interview with best-selling author Ted Dekker, in which he expounds on this theme as his deepest motivation and creative power for writing. He has great insights into the power of story and how his success presented an obstacle, and then a gift, in finding his place within the larger story. Ted Dekker, Interview with Kevin Kaiser, "Sell Out: A Discussion on the Hidden Secret to Writing," *NoiseTrade*, n.d., books.noisetrade.com/teddekker/sell-out-the-hidden-secret-to, Accessed 11 Apr. 2017.

my american life

All the ways of a man are pure in his own eyes,
but the Lord weighs the spirit (Proverbs 16:2).

I GREW UP IN Georgetown, Texas, a suburb of Austin, which was the only place I lived from 18 months old until college. Today, Georgetown is one of the fastest growing cities in the United States.[1] In the Georgetown I grew up in, one could drive anywhere in town within 10 minutes, and the grand opening of Taco Bell was so monumental that searchlights lit up the sky announcing the town's progress.

Georgetown's people lived in rhythm. Local businesses sponsored Little League baseball teams. As the one mascot for all schools, Georgetown Eagles paraphernalia appeared in front yards, business windows, and public offices. Many of the town's residents descended upon San Gabriel Park for Friday night football games and Fourth of July fireworks. Even at an early age, my friends and I roamed the neighborhood without supervision or concern for safety. We rode bikes, played football in the streets, and swam in the local river. In the summer, we played baseball. In the fall, we played basketball or football. On Saturdays, we had ball games. On Sundays, we attended church.

Church
A stable Christian community surrounded me. Church functioned as our second home. I grew up learning the Bible, being mentored

by others, and having a community of peers—who, for the most part—loved God and lived moral lives.

From what I remember, the first time I listened to a sermon in church instead of enduring one was when I was seven. I was bothered. My sin weighed on me as heavily as sin can at that age, but I saw hope in the Bible's message. Jesus would forgive my sins. I believed. And I prayed alongside my parents for Jesus to come into my life.

Apart from a short-lived rebellion in the fifth grade, I never wanted to rebel. I liked being good and did not want to disappoint my parents or others. I started reading the Bible every day in seventh grade and eventually led Christian organizations at church and school. I never smoked, drank alcohol, attended wild parties, or felt social persecution because of my faith. I remained in an "in crowd" at school, and I was never forced to oppose my culture to meet the behavioral expectations of a good Christian.

In my small-town America, however, the real center of my Christian life was me. I asked God to come into my life and bless what I was doing. I viewed God and this world through the lens of what I wanted, and what was best for me.

"All a person's ways seem pure to them, but motives are weighed by the Lord,"[2] the Bible says. My mentors taught me specific boundaries of right and wrong. Consequently, I defined my behavior as pleasing to God if I stayed within the boundaries of what was "right." My ways seemed pure because I obeyed what others taught me. I wonder how much I obeyed, though, because I wanted the approval of others, not because I wanted to serve God or his larger purpose.

I took steps to follow God because I knew I needed what he provided, but like many people, my view of God was bent toward him making my life better. Of course, he can and does improve lives, but as I later discovered, my view of God was limited, and inviting Jesus into my life was part of my problem.

Family

I am the first child of my parents and the first grandchild on both sides of my family. My parents valued family and financial stability.

I never heard them fight, and though they disciplined my brother and me, it was never harsh. This close-knit family extended to loving grandparents, aunts, uncles, and cousins. Only after leaving home have I come to realize how unusual this warm cocoon is in America.

The security of a strong Christian family, a supportive community, and a modest but well-provided lifestyle seemed normal to me. I can now see how these secure assurances were unusual in America, and although they were positive, they were also boundaries that prevented me from seeking more from God.

College

When I left for college, I left my family, my church, and life's familiar patterns, but I did not leave my desire for people's approval. So long as I didn't violate my own sense of right and wrong, I followed what people asked and expected of me. My "Christian life" at a Christian university was easily maintained by following the culture around me.

During my first year of college, however, on a dirty parking lot in Abilene, Texas, my life changed as I began grappling with purpose, cultural expectations, the life of Jesus, and a challenge to obey what—even to this day—seems crazy.

---

[1] According to the U.S. Census, the population of Georgetown within city limits was 9,468 in 1980, 14,842 in 1990, and 28,339 in 2000. Among cities with a population of at least 50,000, Georgetown, TX had the highest percent change of population growth in the United States from 2014 to 2015. Georgetown now has a population of over 60,000 people. Alexa Ura and Annie Daniel, "Texas Suburbs Among Fastest Growing Cities," *The Texas Tribune*, 19 May 2016, www.texastribune.org/2016/05/19/texas-suburbs-among-fastest-growing-cities-us/, Accessed 13 June 2016.

[2] Proverbs 16:2 New International Version.

the parking lot

3

Then Jesus told his disciples, "If anyone would come after me, let him deny himself and take up his cross and follow me. For whoever would save his life will lose it, but whoever loses his life for my sake will find it" (Matthew 16:24-25).

IT WAS NEAR THE end of my first semester at university in Abilene, Texas. I went to a local park to read the Bible and pray. Soon after, I noticed a man sitting in his van nearby, and I felt God leading me to tell the man about Jesus. Approaching a stranger, though, felt awkward. So instead, I placed my large Bible with the words "Holy Bible" facing out for him to see. I paced beside him and sat down to read in front of his vehicle. I justified to myself that if God wanted me to talk to this man, my open display of religiosity would provoke him to leave his van to start a conversation with me. I waited. Within minutes, the man rolled up his window, started up his car, and drove away.

I felt dissonance in my life. On the one hand, my whole world seemed Christian. I grew up in church, I was a good kid, I felt as if my beliefs aligned with the Bible, and I satisfied the expectations of my Christian peers and church family. On the other hand, when I read about Jesus in the Bible, I discovered a Jesus less sanitized and more radical than the one I knew.

The Jesus of the Bible raised his friend from the dead—simultaneously inciting people to believe in him and others to plot his death to preserve their way of life. If the latter did not kill Jesus, they reasoned, "everyone" would believe in him. If belief in Jesus spread, the uproar would provoke Roman authorities to destroy their temple and threaten their semi-autonomous nation.[1] The religious leaders of the day—the "godly" people of the day—wanted to kill Jesus so that their position in society, security, and way of life would remain. I had long viewed Jesus as someone who came to ease and improve my life, not as one who could disrupt my life. Would I still be a follower of Jesus if my life did not become easier or more secure?

As I read the gospels, I saw that Jesus fought the status quo of religiosity. Jesus chastised the Pharisees—religious leaders of the time known for their holiness and piety—for cleaning the outsides of cups and dishes but having the inside of their lives filled with greed and evil (Luke 11:39). On another occasion, he called religious leaders whitewashed tombs that appeared beautiful on the outside but were full of death and dirt on the inside (Matthew 23:37).

Jesus drove vendors from the temple with a whip because they treated God's temple as a place of profit rather than one of prayer (John 2:15). A rich man boasted he fulfilled God's law, yet the same man turned away after Jesus challenged him to sell his possessions to give to the poor (Matthew 19:21).

Jesus always seemed to think differently than the culture around him. When a Jewish crowd saw Jesus's miracle of multiplying food, they became convinced he was the promised Messiah for their people—and their people alone. They clamored to make him their king, yet Jesus slipped away to the hills to be alone (John 6:15). "My kingdom is not of this world," he said (John 18:36).

Through story after story, teaching after teaching, I began to see Jesus as a counter-cultural radical not content to simply enter people's lives, but rather to disrupt their lives as they knew them. He invited people into a life and purpose far greater than meeting the norms and expectations of their culture. In the fall semester of my freshman year of college, I experienced that disruption.

The more I thought deeply about Jesus's story, the more I realized my life resembled the religious leaders whom Jesus fought. I came to realize that the primary question I was answering with my life was, "What does my religious culture tell me to do?" and not, "What does God want me to do?"

The Parking Lot

Before I entered a coffee shop one evening with a friend named Sam, I unloaded with tears the burden, confusion, and conviction swirling inside me. Sam listened—nervously—as I rambled and repented. I anguished over how I would sing songs and make confessions of Jesus as Lord, but refuse to talk about him to a person at the park. I confessed my hypocrisy and resolved to obey God when he gave me commands. I began to see that knowledge of God and the Bible is only as useful as the obedience that results. After all, Jesus said, "If you love me, you will keep my commandments" (John 14:15).

I reflected on the radical nature of Jesus and how people's expectations did not determine his identity and actions. Jesus said he only did what he saw the Father doing (John 5:19). I confessed that I could not do anything else with my life but serve God. I embraced the commands of Jesus—radical words such as, "If anyone would come after me, let him deny himself and take up his cross and follow me" (Matthew 16:24). I did not fully grasp what that meant, but I knew my world was shifting from self-orientation to a vague sense of obeying Jesus and making decisions based on his desires.

Sam and I never entered the coffee shop that night. After I finished my confessions and declared my commitment to follow God no matter what he asked of me, the coffee shop—and all of Abilene for that matter—was closed. With nowhere else to go and no words left to say, I started the car and began to leave.

But as I exited the parking lot, my eyes fixed on the trash strewn across the lot. "Pick up the trash," God commanded. "Pick up all of it."

Did I hear an audible voice? Was it a deep impression or stirring within me? All that I can say is the command was clear—if not audible, clear enough to be audible. I had spent the last few hours ranting about the radical nature of following God and vowing to follow and obey him even if doing so seemed crazy. I assumed such vows related to talking to strangers at parks, choosing where to live, or making social and vocational decisions. But picking up trash in a parking lot?!

I did not turn the car around. Who would know anyway? I proceeded onto the street, my mind and heart racing—wrestling—with the command I had received. "It doesn't make any sense! This is crazy! Who does this? What will people think? The parking lot will just be dirty again the next day!"

I advanced no more than 30 yards, when a confident resolve won the short, intense battle in my soul. I knew God was testing me. Would I do what he asked me to do even if doing so seemed crazy? I turned to Sam in the midst of the sudden U-turn and said, "I can't explain this to you right now, but I have to clean up the parking lot." I parked the car.

On my hands and knees in a parking lot that could fit several hundred vehicles, I began picking up cigarette butts and other trash. I cannot remember how long I cleaned. Two hours? Three?

About halfway through, thinking who knows what, Sam joined me and, without a word, began picking up trash with me. By the end, our hands were stained and dirty. For some reason, we knew the cleaning needed to be done by hand. After we had disposed of every cigarette butt and fast food wrapper, Sam and I sat and stared at the trash-free parking lot. We knew the ground would be littered again in a few hours. We knew our work was meaningless to the world—but for us, the space had become holy ground. I think we even took off our shoes.[2]

The Current of God's Guidance

I'm not sure how different my life would be without my parking lot experience, but I suspect drastically. What if I had kept going and not turned around? What if my actions had failed to match my confident vows to the Lord? Would he have given me another chance? Would he have asked me to scrape gum off the bottom of cafeteria tables? Was he testing my faithfulness in small, obscure commands to entrust me with larger responsibilities? I do not know. So much of life consists of small choices that cascade into monumental events. Small acts of obedience are later discovered to be crucial moments God uses in his Superplan.

One day I listened to a sermon in which Tim Keller said, "God's guidance, according to the Bible, is more something that God *does* than something God gives."[3] Instead of God's guidance typically involving specific instructions, Keller states, "You're standing in it. You're in the middle of the current. It's moving you right along. You're being navigated. You just might not think so."

I have met many people who miss out on the current of God's guidance because they wait for specific instructions before stepping into the river. When one cultivates a passion for the passions of God and releases one's life to the current of God's plan, the specifics of God's guidance begin to fall into place. My freshman year, I became more attuned to God's larger story and gained quiet confidence in embracing God in the unpredictable—sometimes tempestuous—path that God had for my life.

Disentangling from Conformity

After my parking lot experience, I disentangled myself from the conformity that defined me. I began reevaluating my routines. I withdrew from many activities that had consumed my time. I did not regularly date again until I met my wife Nichole five and a half years later. Nichole received the first "I love you" I ever said to a girl.

I no longer felt the need to be in the "in crowd" or have alpha leadership roles, so my friends became more diverse, and I took leadership roles that were more obscure—unseen—like coordinating prayer efforts on campus. I had attended my parents' and grandparents' large Southern Baptist churches all my life, so instead of joining a similar church my freshman year, I visited a variety of churches from different denominations to understand—and feel a part of—the larger Body of Christ.

I began to sympathize with others more and sought to understand those different from me. Sometimes doing so ended comically. One time, my friend Dan and I decided we needed to become homeless for a night to empathize with the homeless. So, one chilly evening, we put on raggedy clothes—which Dan had a surplus of for some reason—rolled around in the dirt, and headed to the streets of Abilene. We walked the railroad tracks, ending up on "the other side of the tracks" where we encountered people who looked as worn and smelled as bad as we did.

We were shocked by the solidarity we felt with them. One man, whom we assumed was homeless due to his disheveled appearance and inebriation, offered us a place to stay at his home. Although we declined, we felt something powerful in the role reversal of being offered benevolence by someone we would usually avoid. Oh, what Jesus gave up, became, and must have felt when he entered into this world and wandered Judea and Galilee without a home among people with more earthly status and pomp than he!

We moved on from that man to shuffle through the sidewalks of downtown Abilene. A man in a tuxedo and his date scurried to the other side of the road when they noticed our paths would cross. We felt less human—our "otherness"—as the sight of us repulsed, discomforted, and frightened these strangers. We found an alleyway to hide from reproving eyes and made a fire in a metal trashcan.

Deep into the night, we found a bridge to sleep under. We lay on cardboard on a slope of dirt and debris, trying not to think about the cold. Dan and I had vowed to endure the streets the whole night without returning home, but as the night grew colder, our backs stiffened and bodies shivered. Dan tossed and turned without sleep. I was nowhere close to sleep either—miserable, yet motionless. Finally, after a few hours of attempting homelessness, I turned to Dan and asked him if he was ready to return. He could not have agreed any faster.

The streets of Abilene are quiet at night, but as we walked back to campus, a car screeched around the corner and sped toward us. A window rolled down revealing a gun. Before we could react, we heard, "Pow! Pow! Pow!" I felt stings on my leg and looked through the darkness at liquid trickling down my thigh. "I've been shot! I've been shot!" I shouted. Dan had come out unscathed and started picking me up to rush me to who knows where. That is, until we stepped into the light. The ooze flowing down my leg was bright yellow and green. I had been shot by a high-powered paintball gun!

Misguided or not in our efforts to empathize with the homeless, we returned to campus to tell the tale—vacillating between laughs of relief and sober thoughts of the vulnerability of the homeless, and of our need to better relate to "the other."

Leaving the Christian Bubble

Though I was determined to escape conformity to my Christian bubble of existence, I found it was not so easy.

My desire not to conform to others' social expectations and my increased yearning to see the world led to a sophomore year in which, at times, I felt isolated and depressed. I was relocating my identity in relationship to Jesus and not in how I related to the culture around me—and at times that felt lonely. I considered leaving Abilene after that year and attending a larger state school. When making major decisions, I have often sought the counsel of many. Proverbs 15:22 claims, "Without counsel plans fail, but with many advisers they succeed." A childhood mentor discouraged me from leaving Abilene. He emphasized that college friendships often last a lifetime and that I should commit to developing some strong relationships I had made. I decided to stay, but my world was changing. Even my best friend Dan was preparing to get married, so I wondered what lay ahead.

Not long after I made that decision, I learned of a partnership between my school and Cambridge University in England. Cambridge selected honors students from our university and a dozen others to attend school in the U.K. for a year with no expense beyond our American school's tuition, room, and board.

The program required high academic scores, and because I entered college without taking life too seriously, my freshman-year grades were below honors level. Even though I did not meet the academic requirements, I still applied. I remember a geology class in which I needed to make a final grade of "A" to have hopes of meeting Cambridge's standards. Somehow, undeservedly, I finished the course with the grade I needed.

The next year, I found myself in the current of God's guidance attending one of the best universities in the world at no more cost than staying in Abilene. Even more extraordinary is how God spoke through two Japanese colleagues at Cambridge to reveal a plan and theme for my life that remain to this day.

---

[1] "If we allow him to go on like this, soon everyone will believe in him. Then the Roman army will come and destroy both our Temple and our nation" (John 11:48).

[2] When the Lord spoke to Moses through a burning bush, God said, "Do not come near; take your sandals off your feet, for the place on which you are standing is holy ground" (Exodus 3:5).

[3] Tim Keller, "Your Plans: God's Plans," *Gospel in Life*, 12 Dec. 2004, www.gospelinlife.com/your-plans-god-s-plans-5394, Accessed 6 July 2016.

Cambridge 4

I make it my ambition to preach the gospel, not where Christ has already been named, lest I build on someone else's foundation, but as it is written, "Those who have never been told of him will see, and those who have never heard will understand" (Romans 15:20-21).

THE SUMMER BEFORE I left for Cambridge, I worked long hours to save money for travel. After arriving in Cambridge, these extra funds enabled me to see as much of Europe as possible. Purchasing a Eurail pass allowed me to hop on and off high-speed trains; I left cities like Barcelona one day, woke up in Nice the next, and proceeded to Geneva that afternoon.

Traveling with only a hiker's backpack, I met fascinating people along the way. An Irishman initiated a conversation with me one day, and proceeded to tell me about his life of crime, escape to Spain, and fugitive life. Australian adventurers abounded, often working odd jobs in various cities for months at a time to pay for their travel. While I sometimes traveled alone, I most often traveled or met up with others. My 18-year-old brother joined me for a couple of weeks on a tour of six countries—taking in the panic of Y2K in Florence.

I mainly traveled with other "junior-year abroad" participants from Cambridge. Two female students accompanied me across the Strait of Gibraltar to Tangier, Morocco, and down to Marrakesh. In Marrakesh, we sipped addicting green tea infused with sugar and fresh mint. We also tried our hand at snake charming cobras.

After a couple of days exploring the city, however, my co-ed companions didn't want to leave the hotel. On a couple of occasions, men had groped them in crowded markets. The way the men treated them made them uncomfortable and terrified of stepping outside. Picking up on their emotions, I never wanted to return to a Muslim or African country again—a sentiment that turned out to be highly ironic.

Instead of residing in an all-male dorm where female visitation was prohibited, as was the case at my Christian university, I lived on a co-ed floor at Cambridge.[1] Men and women were even required to share the bathroom. Except for two adventurous Japanese girls, everyone on the floor was American. All of them were bright and disciplined, but for the first time in my life I lived close to a handful of people who did drugs, slept around, and drank too much. As a follower of Christ learning to relate to a more diverse world, such experiences were helpful for me in living out my convictions but also relating well to those with different lifestyles.

The Limits of Knowledge

While I found my travels enriching, nothing stimulated me more than the academic atmosphere of Cambridge. For the first time, I loved learning. I have never had a more fruitful year of academics than the year I spent in England. In the past, as an unintended consequence of the education model I grew up with, I finished assignments and studied content in order to pass examinations. At Cambridge, they had little concern for tests and grades; they simply wanted us to learn. I remember turning in my first essay thinking I would receive it back the next week with a grade. Instead, we met with professors alone or with a few other students to defend our essays.

More often than not, the professors explained where we grasped key concepts but returned our papers with pointers to strengthen our arguments. They then assigned reading to help us better understand the topic. We returned two to four weeks later with our strengthened essays only to receive similar instructions again. By the end of the class, we had produced solid work and knew the content well enough to engage in meaningful dialogue with our professors.

I studied church history, theology, bioethics, sociology, educational psychology, sculpture, archaeology, and literature. I considered a future in academics—of becoming an expert on a subject like my professors. As the year continued, however, I began seeing another side to academic pursuits and travel adventures.

In my tutorials with world-renowned church historians and theologians, some of them confessed to me the emptiness in their souls. The prevailing posture of criticism when approaching the biblical text, some admitted, had slowly stamped out the vibrant faith of their youth. We regularly prayed for some of our theology professors before tutorials!

Through the academic process, human capacity and capability had been elevated to the point that some professors had no use or need for God. Critical thinking and the trust in humanity's ability to reason apart from faith or relationship with a living God led some professors to obtain educational expertise—which they most valued—only to find despair within the limitations of reason. One can never know enough! The pursuit of knowledge divorced from faith is a meandering trail of hopelessness for finding purpose.

My interactions with some of these troubled professors reinforced my belief that knowing God and the Bible requires active faith, relationship, and obedience. By the end of the year, I realized that academic achievement and the adventure of travel could become objects of devotion and alternative forms of self-centered living.

Never Met a Christian

Within the diversity of my co-ed dorm floor, I started a prayer meeting and Bible study. The two Japanese girls on my floor, Himari and Kanna, became good friends and showed interest in the Bible. They often attended church with me. They came to prayer meetings and Bible studies. They were present when I shared my spiritual journey as a follower of Jesus on the campus's main lawn at a Christian event. Although friendly and talkative, Himari and Kanna rarely shared their emotions or beliefs. Toward the end of our year in England, I separately asked them about what they had learned at the Christian meetings.

Himari, the more outspoken of the two, said, "I love hearing about Jesus, and I like Christians. I wish I could become a follower of Jesus, but if I did so, I would bring shame upon my family and myself. Furthermore, I have never met a Christian in Japan."

A few days later, I asked my friend Kanna, the more introspective one, the same question. "Ohhh, Chris," she explained, "Christians always talk about love. Love God with your whole heart, soul, and mind. Love your neighbor as yourself. I find this hard to understand because there is no word for love as you describe it in my language. Furthermore, I have never met a Christian in Japan."

We finished out the year. Himari and Kanna returned to Japan, and I returned to America. I made plans to visit them but lacked the funds to do so. And we soon lost contact.

Despite our paths diverging, when Himari and Kanna said they couldn't follow Jesus because of never meeting a Christian in Japan, they changed my life forever.

Understanding God's Mission

When I returned to Abilene my senior year, I completed the required classes for my psychology major. Throughout the year, the words of my Japanese friends in England haunted me. They had never met a Christian in their country. All the while, I lived in a city where Christian churches appeared on almost every corner.

On my own time, apart from school classes, I devoted myself to understanding the mission of God. I began reading biographies of those who gave up comfortable lives to live out the message of Jesus among peoples who had not heard. Hudson Taylor, a 19th-century missionary who lived on faith in God and faced social criticism from fellow missionaries for his efforts to enculturate the message of Jesus into Chinese culture, became a hero. I regularly looked at and reflected upon pictures and quotes from Mother Teresa. She remarked, "While in the slums, we see Christ and touch him in the broken bodies, in the abandoned children."[2] Her life, so identified with and poured out for the "least of these," inspired and challenged me to do the same in another culture.

Familiar Bible verses and stories jumped out at me with new meaning. When Abraham received his blessing from God, it was not only for promised land and to be the father of a great nation, but his blessing was also that through him "all peoples on earth will be blessed" (Genesis 12:3 New International Version)[3]—not just his people, but all the peoples of the world. Jesus gave what we call the Great Commission: "Go therefore and make disciples of all nations" (Matthew 28:19), but I never realized that the nations Jesus referred to were more numerous than the modern world's geopolitical countries such as Iraq, China, Nigeria, or the United States. Jesus used the Greek word *ethne*, which can be translated as ethnic groups or people groups. Go make disciples of all the ethnic groups—of all the peoples.[4] The people groups in the world to-day number around 16,500[5] compared to around 200 geopolitical countries. I assumed the Body of Christ had been making disciples in all the countries of the world, but 16,500 people groups?

When I studied the global Church's progress in following Jesus's command, I found that over 40% of the world's people groups were still considered unreached—having little or no Christian wit-ness—2,000 years after Christ died and rose again.[6] I discovered my Japanese friends were not anomalies when I later heard that 86% of the world's Muslims, Hindus, and Buddhists do not know a Christian.[7] Himari and Kanna's experience of not knowing any Christians was shockingly normal, and God was using them to jolt me out of my self-focused life. God was unveiling the theme and direction he had for me—"to be the one Christian someone knows."

---

[1] Cambridge University consists of around 30 different undergraduate college campuses. I resided at Homerton College but took classes at various campuses.

[2] Mother Teresa, *Love, a Fruit Always in Season* (San Francisco: Ignatius Press, 1987) 151.

[3] "I will make you into a great nation, and I will bless you; I will make your name great, and you will be a blessing. I will bless those who bless you, and whoever curses you I will curse; and all peoples on earth will be blessed through you" (Genesis 12:2-3 New International Version). "To your offspring I will give this land" (Genesis 12:7). Those who have faith in Christ are blessed through the Abrahamic covenant and are, likewise, called to carry on the blessing to all peoples. "Know then that it is those of faith who are the sons of Abraham. And the Scripture, foreseeing that God would justify the Gentiles by faith, preached the gospel beforehand to Abraham, saying, 'In you shall all the nations be blessed.' So then, those who are of faith are blessed along with Abraham, the man of faith" (Galatians 3:7-9).

[4] Likewise, in Matthew 24:14, a word using the same root word *ethnos* is used that is typically translated as nation. "And this gospel of the kingdom will be

proclaimed throughout the whole world as a testimony to all *'nations'* (*ethnic groups*), and then the end will come" (emphasis and parenthetical insertion mine). A picture of heaven appears in Revelation 7:9-10: "After this I looked, and behold, a great multitude that no one could number, from every nation, from all tribes and peoples and languages, standing before the throne and before the Lamb, clothed in white robes, with palm branches in their hands, and crying out with a loud voice, 'Salvation belongs to our God who sits on the throne, and to the Lamb!'"

[5] There are different ways to define people groups, so statistics vary. Joshua Project is a respected and widely used people group database. In the summer of 2016, Joshua Project counted 16,510 people groups in the world. "Global Statistics," *Joshua Project*, July 2016, joshuaproject.net/people_groups/statistics, Accessed 15 July 2016. Other popular databases include www.peoplegroups. org and the World Christian Database.

[6] Joshua Project defines an unreached ethnic group as one that is less than 2% evangelical Christian and less than 5% Christian adherent to any other form of Christianity. "Definitions: Unreached/Least-Reached," *Joshua Project*, n.d., joshuaproject.net/help/definitions, Accessed 11 Apr. 2017.

[7] Todd M. Johnson and Kenneth R. Ross, eds., *Atlas of Global Christianity* (Edinburgh: Edinburgh University Press, 2009) 316.

mali

Go therefore and make disciples of all nations,
baptizing them in the name of the Father
and of the Son and of the Holy Spirit (Matthew 28:19).

I LANDED IN BAMAKO, the capital city of Mali, five months after college graduation—and one month after 9/11. Mali had always been a somewhat tolerant country for missionaries and Christians, but that was changing. Osama Bin Laden stickers were plastered on every public transport vehicle.[1] Bin Laden was a celebrity—a hero.

While most Malians would move to America in a heartbeat, this reality was contrasted with Bin Laden's popularity. I had committed my next two years to a people who were venerating the architect of al-Qaeda's assault on America's largest city. I wondered what Bin Laden symbolized to them. The triumph of Islam? Victory for the underdog? Rejection of Western immorality? All I knew was that these were my new neighbors—and that Jesus called me to love my enemies, and pray for those who persecute me (Matthew 5:44).

Becoming a Missionary

Mali had not been my first choice. Because of the influence of my Japanese friends and missionary heroes such as Hudson Taylor, I expected to leave Texas for Japan or China.

After college graduation, I attended a conference to select a missionary position overseas. While waiting in line to talk to representatives from China and Japan, a man I did not know tapped me on the shoulder and said the West Africa representative was praying for me specifically about moving to West Africa. I looked at the long line in front of me, looked back at the strange man who tapped me on the shoulder, then looked at the empty table of those interested in West Africa. I decided to hear him out.

The West Africa representative shared a boring job description of handling logistics for American volunteers on short-term mission trips in Mali. I had never heard of Mali. It sounded exotic—like Bali or Maui—but it was actually a land-locked country full of Sahara sand and home to Timbuktu, a place synonymous with the "end of the world." I was not interested. "Pray about it," he said. I agreed to do so.

Over the next few days of consultation and prayer, I felt less peace about moving to Asia and a surprising peace about moving to Mali. In seeking God's will, sometimes people confuse the peace of God with comfort. I did not feel comfortable. I felt the peace of God clarifying my direction. I had no emotional ties or inherent interest in Mali to cloud my judgment. I knew the move would be difficult, but if I did not go, I knew I would be disobedient to God. I felt at peace with his guidance.

My job assignment was leading American volunteers to minister among the dozens of Malian people groups with little or no Christian presence. Since I did not feel qualified for the "real missionary" positions of church planting, teaching at seminaries, developing agricultural programs, and the like, I warmed up to the idea of guiding volunteers.

Overwhelmed

Immersion in a culture and language starkly different from one's own is unnatural and humiliating. So much of our identity is determined by what we achieve or by maintaining social expectations within a group—neither of which occurs when first entering and learning another culture or language. At the time I arrived, Mali was the fourth least developed country in the world, and my ministry team spent over half of our time in remote villages. I was from one of the richest and most developed countries on earth, seeking to relate to people whose language and way of living I did not know. I was productive in America, but when I arrived in Mali, I had no ability to communicate, no relevant skills to contribute, and little common ground with the people. Furthermore, I accepted a position in Mali to coordinate American volunteers, most of whom canceled their trips due to post-9/11 fear of Muslims.

I had heard of new missionaries emotionally breaking down in Mali due to the onslaught of culture shock, language difficulty, and the stress of leaving their sense of identity and belonging to live in a religious culture so different than their own. One missionary frequently spent his first few months in the fetal position longing for home. Another missionary had nervous breakdowns for an entire year. Every few weeks in attempts to visit the village, she had to return to the city before, or shortly after, reaching the village due to the difficulty of cultural expectations, sickness, and poverty.

But those are the missionaries who persevered through difficulty. Many other missionaries returned home early, finding the disappointment, shame, or regret in a premature return more comfortable than staying. As the biting sand of a Sahara sandstorm disorients and stings, culture shock so disorients and afflicts missionaries in Mali that many become disillusioned with their calling and leave. None of us were immune. Among the missionary community, we often referred to "ticket days." Sometimes, life felt so hard and our sense of spiritual fortitude so weak, that if we had possessed a return plane ticket, we would have left that day.

One evening, a Malian friend asked me for money for what seemed like the hundredth time. Out of fear of dependency and feeling the emotional weight of the wealth disparity between my Western riches—even on my lowly missionary salary—and his income, I broke down crying as I refused. He looked at me with a confused expression and replied with a pained smile, "You are tired and ill. You need some sleep. Good night." He then slowly shut my apartment door.

I knew God called me to Mali for a reason, and I was determined to endure any emotional or cultural challenge I encountered. But how do people know what they can handle—the limitations of their resilience—until they face the difficulty? I felt inadequate in adjusting to my new culture, and I needed help.

Seba the Butcher

One day, on one of my frequent walks through the dirt streets of my neighborhood, I came across Seba, the neighborhood butcher. Instead of having his own store with pre-cut beef, neatly packed, chilled, and separated by type of cut, Seba hung a beef carcass above a wooden table at the end of my dusty, sweltering street. When customers ordered beef, Seba took his butcher knife, chopped a slab of meat and bone off the carcass, placed the selection on the cardboard-covered table, hacked away to obtain the desired amount, and weighed the meat and bone on a balance scale to charge the customer per kilogram. He performed this operation on a beef carcass covered in flies. I never bought meat from Seba.

Nevertheless, the more I interacted with him, the more I realized Seba unusually connected with me and helped me. Ironically, he was the person in my middle-class Malian neighborhood with whom I had the least in common. He had only received a third-grade education. He was unable to read or write. He made a pittance selling meat 60 hours a week. And he couldn't speak French, the "white man's language," which many people spoke in my neighborhood. When I began greeting Seba, however, he took special interest in me and wanted me to learn his people's language and culture.

At first, we just laughed at each other as we sat on wood-carved stools and attempted to communicate, him in his village Bambara unadulterated by French, and I in my efforts to practice every Bambara word I had learned. I discovered new words with him as we played charades in attempts to communicate—chirping like chickens with flapping arms and performing other child-like demonstrations in desperation to connect.

Seba was patient, but tough. He made me work and practice. He cared that I understood nuanced meaning in the language and why their culture had certain beliefs and practices. While swatting flies and hacking at the beef carcass, Seba raised me in the culture and language. When I was in the city, we spent at least three hours together each day as I worked through the headaches and mental fatigue of immersion in Bambara. I learned to converse by being raised in the language like an infant, not by books and grammar. After a while, I began visiting Seba's home and became friends with his family and neighbors. His courtyard became my second home. He corrected me, chastised me, nurtured me, and advised me. I was a baby in the culture and language, and he raised me like a son of Mali.

Most Malians loved to talk about religion. Because I came to Mali to share the love of Jesus with people, this Malian disposition toward religious conversation fit well. An unusual characteristic of my relationship with Seba, however, was that he never wanted to talk about religion, my faith in Jesus, or my motivation for moving to Mali. Since he made this clear, we avoided the subject, until his own child became ill.

One evening, several months into our relationship, we sat outside his courtyard drinking tea. He looked at me with concern and pleaded, "I need you to pray for my son—he is very sick." He did not add details. For all I knew, his son had nothing more than a headache. I told Seba I would pray right then. I explained that Jesus had the ability to heal people if he chose, and I prayed for Jesus to heal Seba's son. My prayer was simple, no different from the prayer one utters in church while glancing at prayer requests for the sick.

A couple of days later, however, when I took a routine visit to his courtyard, Seba rushed to my vehicle with joy. He took me by the hand and thanked me profusely. He explained that he thought his child was going to die[2]—details I was unaware of—but when I prayed for his son in Jesus's name, his son was healed. For the next couple of hours, my friend and cultural parent, who had refused to talk about religion, took me to every friend he had in the neighborhood and greeted them in the following way: "This is my American friend who prayed in the name of Jesus, and my son was healed." Over and over, he repeated the introduction: "This is my American friend who prayed in the name of Jesus, and my son was healed." To another, he said, "This is my American friend. He prayed in the name of Jesus, and my son was healed."

From that moment forward, in every lengthy visit with Seba, he wanted to talk about Jesus and the Bible. Later, I introduced a Malian follower of Jesus to Seba's compound, and a Malian-led Bible study began. As a result, at least one Muslim man became a follower of Christ. God began to show me he could use me in my weakness and inadequacy to carve out a path far different and worthwhile than the path I would have chosen. After all, God gave me a linguistic and cultural parent who was an uneducated butcher with no interest in the Bible to help me relate to Malian people and open doors for the message of Jesus to the 50 people in his courtyard. But divine plot twists are common in God's Superplan, something I experienced again when a Muslim man revealed his dream about Jesus, and me.

---

[1] Before the veneration of Bin Laden increased, however, the government of Mali began fining drivers the equivalent of one U.S. dollar if they kept Bin Laden stickers on their vehicle. Most stickers disappeared overnight.

[2] At the time I lived in Mali, the country had one of the highest infant mortality rates in the world. In 2001, 23% of Malian children died before the age of five. "Nutrition of Young Children and Mothers: Mali 2001," *The DHS Program* (Calverton, MD: ORC Macro, Sep. 2002), dhsprogram.com/pubs/pdf/ANC9/ML-01ChartBookEng.pdf, Accessed 23 July 2016.

omar's dream 6

Then the angel showed me the river of the water of life, as clear as crystal, flowing from the throne of God and of the Lamb down the middle of the great street of the city. On each side of the river stood the tree of life, bearing twelve crops of fruit, yielding its fruit every month. And the leaves of the tree are for the healing of the nations (Revelation 22:1-2).

BECAUSE OF 9/11, AMERICAN churches were afraid to send volunteer teams to Muslim countries like Mali, so I spent only a small amount of my time fulfilling my job description as a volunteer coordinator. Instead, I had conversations in Bambara with people in their homes and on the streets for hours each day. I began leading a Bible study in Bambara after two months in the country. My language ability at that point was limited, but I progressed quickly and started multiple Bible studies with interested Muslims. Although I would never have moved to Mali as an evangelist or church planter, I began growing into those roles.

With massive unemployment, Mali's capital city of Bamako teemed with groups of men who sipped tea and talked all day. Even among strangers, the custom in Mali is to greet passersby in a lengthy and rhythmic greeting. "Did you sleep with peace in the night?" "Only peace." "Are you well?" "No problems." "Is your wife well?" "No problems." "Are your children well?" "Absolutely no problems." And so on. Once the first person finishes with questions, the roles reverse with a similar set of questions and answers before closing with, "May we meet again," or, "May God keep us together."

As a result, I greeted many people on the streets whom I never engaged further in conversation. Omar was one of those people. A servant and security guard for my neighbor across the street,

Omar's face seemed fixed in a smile. For months, we exchanged polite greetings but did not talk further.

One day, however, Omar asked me a pointed question: "Why do you never talk to me about Jesus and the Bible?"

Of course, there was no significant reason for excluding Omar from such conversations, but I replied, "Oh, are you interested in Bible and Jesus conversations? We can do that. I am sorry for not sitting and conversing with you."

"That's okay," he replied. "Yes, we need to talk. I want to know about Jesus and the Bible."

We arranged a time to visit on Omar's day off. Based on his interest, I planned to take the full day to tell the overarching story of the Bible, starting with Creation and working our way through Abraham, Moses, David, and the other prophets with whom Muslims were familiar. I planned on laying a foundation for Omar with God's love for humanity, humanity's sin and rebellion in following their own way instead of God's, the consequences of humanity's sin, and God's promised provision of blessing for those who had faith in him. If we took the full day to cover these stories, I determined to start the stories of Jesus the following week if he remained interested.

Omar came to my apartment, and we began as planned. For the entire morning, I shared stories of the prophets, played recordings of native Bambara-speakers sharing the stories, and discussed them with Omar. The stories of these first prophets are similar to accounts Muslims read in the Qur'an, so discussing such texts in the Bible often builds a bridge before introducing, for them, the confrontational and unfamiliar claims and teachings of Jesus. When Omar and I stopped for lunch, however, he looked at me with frustration.

"When are we going to talk about Jesus?" he asked. "I want to hear about Jesus."

I had never heard a Muslim express such interest in Jesus—especially on an initial visit. I explained why we started with the Bible's foundational stories, but replied, "I can summarize what took place so we can move on to the stories of Jesus."

"That would be good," he said. He fidgeted in his chair, and his eyes shifted from one side to another. Finally, he made eye contact with me, then stared at the table below him and said, "I had a dream."

"A dream? Tell me about it," I said.

He leaned in and began:

You know the other day, after you shared some from the Bible after I asked? That night I had a dream. In the dream, a group of Malians stood around you, myself included. We were by a river. But the river was different. It was white and clear, and it glowed.[1] A voice came from the river and asked me, "Who is your friend standing beside you?"

I replied, "This is my friend Mamadou (which is my African name)."

"He is a good person," the voice told me. "Listen to what he says about Jesus the Son. Accept this as the truth. Omar, do not let this go."

And then the dream ended.

I listened in amazement to Omar's story. I was the only Christian Omar knew and he was asking me how to become a follower of Jesus.

I had heard of Muslims dreaming about Jesus. Now, Omar was describing a dream in which God told him to listen to my words about Jesus. That day, I altered my carefully planned series of Bible stories. I told Omar of humanity's need of being cleansed from our sin, of how we cannot come to God with our plans or religion but have to come to him as he prescribes. I told Omar of God's gift in sending Jesus as a sacrifice to cleanse our sins and provide the way to Paradise.

That evening, Omar accepted the gift of God through Jesus and exclaimed, "Today, today has become a party—because today I found God."

Beyond the Compound

During my first months in Mali, when not traveling to villages, I lived in an apartment below my organization's office behind a locked door. Beyond the locked door was a foyer secured by a set of chained doors. Beyond the chained doors lay a landscaped courtyard with a giant mango tree and the constant watch of a security guard. Surrounding the courtyard stood a tall, thick wall with razor wire and two secured gates that opened to the street. Not long after Omar's dream and commitment to follow Jesus, my organization informed me I needed to move from my apartment. Instead of assigning me a new home, they asked for my input on where I wanted to live.

Faced with imposed opportunity, I could either choose another comfortable, safe place to live, or I could move beyond secured walls to live among the people I had come to love. I asked God, "Where do you want me to live? I asked myself, "What about Jesus—the nonconforming, radical, obedient Son of the Father? Where would Jesus choose to live?"

Immediately, I thought of Omar, who was single at the time. I envisioned living with him in his impoverished neighborhood and starting a church in his courtyard. But when I asked the question, "God, where do you want me to live?" it was an open-ended question. I asked a question with room for God to take me where he desired—not necessarily to where I expected, and not necessarily to a place that fit into my organization's structure or plans.

---

[1] The river in Omar's dream resembles one described in Revelation 22:1-2: "Then the angel showed me the river of the water of life, bright as crystal, flowing from the throne of God and of the Lamb through the middle of the street of the city."

7

Wassoulou

You are the light of the world. A city set on a hill cannot be hidden. Nor do people light a lamp and put it under a basket, but on a stand, and it gives light to all in the house. In the same way, let your light shine before others, so that they may see your good works and give glory to your Father who is in heaven (Matthew 5:14-16).

WHERE SHOULD MISSIONARIES, OR people in God's Superplan, live? This basic question has been a point of tension since the modern missionary enterprise began. Should missionaries from outside the culture keep their home a haven? Should missionaries create a sanctuary to withstand culture shock and keep themselves on the mission field? Or should missionaries attempt to live and dress like the people they work among, trying to expunge their cultural preferences to disassociate foreignness from the conveyed message of Jesus Christ? And if so, are the missionaries being genuine and true to themselves? The answers to such questions have led to frequent tensions between missionaries.

Hudson Taylor, the famed 19th-century missionary to China, was convinced mission work should not be confined to Western missionary compounds. He advocated for missionaries to push toward the interior of China and take on Chinese dress and customs. His sentiment infuriated many of his peers who counted the spread of "their superior culture" as an integrated mission with the spread of the gospel.

Hudson Taylor's thoughts do not seem radical now, but at the time, Chinese who showed interest in the gospel most often had to enter the missionary's milieu instead of the other way around—even on their own soil. As a result, the Chinese who became Christians took on status as outsiders and foreigners within their communities.

Hudson Taylor wanted to change that scenario. Since he diverged from the norms of missionary culture at the time, his colleagues opposed and slandered him.

Miss Aldersey, reputed to be the first woman missionary in China, was influential and contemptuous toward Taylor—partly because he donned Chinese dress. When hearing of Hudson Taylor's desire to marry a young girl for whom she acted as a guardian, Miss Aldersey denounced Taylor as a "young, poor, unconnected nobody."[1] She further derided him as, "called by no one, connected with no one, recognized by no one as a minister of the gospel, fanatical, undependable, diseased in body and mind, and totally worthless!"[2] And she was not the only one opposed to Taylor's methods for making the gospel message more accessible to the Chinese.

Although not as extreme, I wrestled with the same issues. I had moved to Bamako eight months prior. I had spent many hours with people on the streets and in their homes. I had enjoyed my frequent trips to the village in which I was in the constant presence of adults and hounded by children. I had loved hanging out with people.

Nevertheless, I had taken frequent respites in my sanctuary in the city—escapes into my American cave stocked with taco shells, Dr. Pepper, and Internet connection to home.[3] When the disruption came to choose a new place to live, I was prodded to evaluate where God wanted me to live. If I stayed in a similar apartment, I could continue to escape from discomfort when desired. When irritable, ill, or homesick, I could retreat and emerge on the outside when at my ministry best. As a missionary, I felt as if I needed to "be on" all the time, and that I should only see people when I had something to give. Upon reflection, I realized my apartment buffered me from being vulnerable with my Malian friends and neighbors.

The One who called me to be the "one Christian someone knows" and sent me to Mali, however, is the One who "emptied himself, by taking the form of a servant, being born in the likeness of men. And being found in human form, he humbled himself by becoming obedient to the point of death, even death on a cross" (Philippians 2:7-8).

Jesus took on the vulnerability of human flesh and was the incarnation of God and his message. Instead of preparing lessons behind a wall and coming out to share them when prepared, Jesus's life was the message. He had no home. He healed the sick. He wept in front of people. He had compassion for the poor. And he taught lessons as he walked, dined, and conversed with people. Lessons came naturally as he pointed people's life situations toward the Kingdom of God. Jesus took illustrations from what he saw around him—fishermen, farmers, seed, salt, and a city on a hill. The power of Jesus's message was touched and felt, something that was diminished if it was prepared behind walls topped with razor-wire. I came to realize that Christ's light in me was not simply for my benefit; it was also a part of his message *to others*.

"You are the light of the world," Jesus claimed. Therefore, "Let your light shine before others" (Matthew 5:14,16).

I recognized in Christ's example that God's power emanates from helping and teaching out of a position of vulnerability. My struggles, my pain, and my failures become opportunities to point to Christ's strength in tangible ways, and they would have much more of an effect than polished and prepared forms of teaching.

I began to realize that my role as a missionary is not merely to teach a message, but to live a message—and such a lifestyle meant leaving a walled-off apartment. I first thought of moving in with Omar. His courtyard consisted of several Muslim families in a lower-class neighborhood. As I continued to dream and pray, however, another possibility leaped into my mind and did not leave until I pursued it further.

Moving to Bandogo

On the volunteer trips that our team led, we occasionally visited a people group called the Wassoulou. Located only a couple of hundred kilometers from Bamako in southern Mali, Wassoulou land took the majority of a day to reach on washboard and pot-holed dirt roads.[4] When we talked to Malians in Bamako, they were terrified at the notion of visiting the Wassoulou because of the group's powerful sorcery. We knew of no Jesus-followers among the estimated 140,000 Wassoulou people on the borderlands of Mali, Guinea, and Cote d'Ivoire.

While we visited many different villages, the village chief of Bandogo was most welcoming to us. We stopped at his village on every trip to Wassoulou land even though Bandogo lacked the significance of other villages. Bandogo did not even have a weekly market. But we developed a genuine friendship with the village chief and his family, and God was at work in that village through their openness to our presence and faith.

As I prayed about where to live, I felt a resolve in my heart to move to Bandogo. But my organization had only asked for my input on where I would like to live in Bamako. The actual decision belonged to them. I was a new missionary without status who had answered a job description as a volunteer coordinator. Within my organization, people my age with my missionary status typically assisted grown-up career missionaries. They seldom started mission work among a people group on their own. I was right out of college with a psychology degree!

Nevertheless, I asked my organization if I could move to the village. In God's Superplan, he often asks us to step outside the norms of our organization or culture. Surprisingly, my supervisors affirmed my desire and encouraged me to scout out the possibility.

I left as soon as I could for Bandogo. Upon arrival, the village chief's older brother Soulou greeted me outside his courtyard. I joined him as he drank tea and chatted with village elders. After a while, I leaned toward Soulou—who was wearing a large *boubou*, dark sunglasses, and a knit cap—and asked him, "Soulou, how would it work if an American lived in your village?"

Soulou's eyes widened, he glanced around, then grabbed my hand and led me inside his hut. I noticed an ancient-looking idol carved from wood on the floor. Soulou looked at the hut's entrance to make sure no one stood nearby, then replied to my question, "Mamadou, several people in Bandogo want to become Christian. I know this. I have heard them talking. I know even more people who want to study the Bible." He leaned back in his chair, chuckled, and added, "And I'm one of them."

"What?!" I replied. "Okay, Soulou," I nearly jumped out of my seat. "I am the American thinking about moving to your village. What would that look like?"

We then talked about logistics, and he even offered me a hut in his courtyard. Later that day, when we saw the village chief and discussed possibilities, he insisted I stay with him. "Bad sorcerers live near Soulou," he claimed.

I took several survey trips before moving to Bandogo. On one trip, during the rainy season, the people of Bandogo were despondent because one whole week had passed without rain. Almost everyone in the village farmed for a living.

"What do we do?" they pleaded.

"Well," I replied, "we know God controls the rain, the sky, and all creation. Let us ask him to provide."

Several Christians who accompanied me gathered with family members of the village chief in his compound. The Christians prayed in Jesus's name for the rain to come and for God to provide. Not long after, as the villagers later reminded us, the rain poured. As we waited out the rain before returning to Bamako, we could not complain when the rain destroyed part of the road and delayed our journey home.

Village Life

Any fear I had of living a comfortable life dissipated when I moved to Bandogo. As described at the book's beginning, villagers considered me a wealthy man with my few possessions, and I came with only a small percentage of what I owned. I felt strange and uncomfortable having less income than people in America but, at the same time, having extravagant wealth in my mud hut village. Was I rich? Was I poor? The short answer was, "Yes."

If a Bambara word exists for "privacy," I never heard it in the village. The huts were used for sleeping and to store goods. Almost everything else happened outside. One cooked outside, ate outside, conversed with others outside, showered outside, and even took bowel movements outside in latrines.

In America, I had days when the only time I ventured outside was walking from a parking lot into a building. And I spent a significant amount of my day independent of others. In Bandogo, life was interdependent, and I rarely had moments to myself. Everywhere

I walked, kids flocked to me like children to free ice cream. I held their hands and talked to them until adults shooed them away.

One day, I entered my mud hut to rest and read. Instead of leaving me at the door, six or seven children followed me inside. I told the kids I planned on reading for a while and could not talk. They shrugged their shoulders, sat down on the floor and, apart from occasional whispers and giggles, did nothing but watch me read for an hour. Without electricity in the village, I was the most entertaining thing around. I was their television!

My village morning started before the roosters crowed—which were loud, but nothing compared to the annoying bellow of the courtyard donkey. As the honored guest resident, one of the village chief's two wives knocked on my door every morning before dawn to make sure I was among the first awake.

"Mamadou, Mamadou, i k'i wuli k'i ko!" ("Mamadou, Mamadou, rise and wash yourself!").

Some mornings, one of the wives woke early to warm water for my bucket bath. Some days the water was cold. Either way, the bucket of water waited for me by the designated place to shower— although the site was sometimes used to urinate as well.

The shower area stood on the edge of the courtyard and consisted of mud walls about neck high with a small entryway. Covering the entryway was a ripped rice bag[5] that dangled to the ground from a chopped tree branch. During the cool season, one of my least favorite parts of village life was stripping down in the cool weather, dipping a cup into a bucket of cool water (on the unlucky days it wasn't heated), and pouring it over my shivering body.

Putting on my clean clothes after the bucket bath was an acquired skill. Since the dirt ground below had turned to mud, I needed to balance on one foot, remove my thong sandal from the other foot, and carefully put my pants on one leg at a time without falling to the ground or letting my pants touch the mud. I am not sure how the people in the village did it, but I am sure if they saw my clumsy attempts at dressing, they would still be laughing decades later.

After I dressed, I returned to my hut for a quiet time of prayer and Bible study (one of my rare moments of solitude). I was then expected to walk by the dozens of huts in the village chief's compound and greet everyone—especially the older men.

"Koh, koh, koh," was the sound I used in Bambara that mimicked a door knock. "Good morning! Did you sleep in peace? Are you well? May God multiply peace throughout your day!"

The pageantry of greetings took an hour or so as I presented myself to everyone in the courtyard and ensured everyone was well. One afternoon, one of the elders saw me and grumbled.

"You didn't greet me this morning," he said.

Actually, I had tried calling for him during my morning rounds, but he was old and prone to sleep late.

"I am sorry," I replied. "I came by earlier, but you must have been sleeping. I should have returned to greet you. I have faulted you."

"No problem," he answered, but in case I did not get the message, he said, "You should greet the old men in the courtyard every morning. One day we won't be here anymore."

I replied, "You speak truth, old man. I hear you."

He died within a year.[6]

As I continued my day, I often wandered through the labyrinth of trails that connected courtyards of different families—greeting everyone along the way. Most groups of men pleaded with me to sit for tea and conversation as I passed. I declined politely to some and sat with others. I became an apprentice of sorts to the village baker and the village blacksmith. I walked to the fields with farmers and convinced them to let me help with their backbreaking work. As part of the process of understanding and loving the Wassoulou people, I attempted to do everything the way they did. I ate what they ate. I drank what they drank. I sat with village elders and learned of their ways. Some men involved in secret societies even told me a few of their secrets.

Sorcery

I took notes on what I learned. I discovered how the Wassoulou came into existence 1,000 years earlier. I learned about the founding of Bandogo. I learned that three bad sorcerers lived in the center of the village (who one approached, say, if one were a husband's first wife and wanted to harm a newly acquired second wife), and six good sorcerers lived elsewhere in the village (if one needed help with sickness, fertility, and the like).

One of the good sorcerers was Seydou, my neighbor with whom I enjoyed stimulating conversations. One day, a man with a headache came looking for Seydou as we sat together in the courtyard. Seydou took the man aside, listened to him, asked a few questions, collected a few coins, and sat him down on a stool. My good sorcerer friend wrote a passage from the Qur'an on a tablet, washed the ink off onto the ground with his spittle, ran his fingers through the mud, and rubbed the concoction on the man's forehead while uttering passages from the Qur'an. Seydou told him to come back if the headache persisted, then sent him on his way.

The practice of Islam in Mali resembles the folk Islam practiced by many Muslims in the world. Traditional religious beliefs mix with standard Islamic doctrine. When the pan-African soccer tournament was held in Mali, Cameroon beat Senegal in the final. The next day, the discussion on Malian radio and the streets of Bamako was not the prowess of the Cameroon soccer club, but the prowess of Cameroon sorcerers compared to those from Senegal—which was obviously what determined the match's outcome.

In a country of folk Islam, the Wassoulou are known and feared throughout the country for their sorcery. One class of people among the Wassoulou, the *donso* (hunters), openly sacrifice to idols and are unashamed of being *kafirs* (pagans).

Despite such spiritual bondage, many people in Bandogo disclosed an interest in the message of Jesus and the Bible. Of course, I heard rhetoric common to some Muslims such as, "We hate Christians," "No one would ever leave Islam to become a Christian," and, "I love Jesus and believe he will come back in the end times…to make everyone Muslim." But I was shocked at how open the people of Bandogo were to my presence and the message and power of Jesus.

Finding Purpose

One night, Yacoub, the village chief's younger brother, approached me. After standard greetings and light conversation, he said, "I want to know how to become a Christian."

At the time, I was not holding any Bible studies or doing any overt evangelism. I was simply present among the people of Bandogo. I told them, sincerely, that I wanted to learn about their ways and that I would seek God's wisdom in how to contribute to village life. I knew I needed to listen and learn before I had anything to give. Nevertheless, people sought me out to learn about Jesus. I happened to be the only Christian nearby who they could approach.

Yacoub continued, "I had a Christian friend once when I lived in Cote d'Ivoire. I learned a lot from him. But no one has ever told me how to become a Christian."

A few days later, a young adult in the courtyard confessed, "I believe the way of Christians is true. You need to teach me."

"Why do you believe this?" I asked.

He said:

Well, we perform our sacrifices, and God doesn't answer. We pray the Muslim prayers, and God doesn't answer. But when Christians pray, God answers. Look, everyone knows, when it doesn't rain in Mali, the government calls upon the religious people of the country to pray. It never rains on the Muslim day of the week, but it always rains on the Christian day of the week.

This person also happened to be present when our small gathering of Christians prayed for the rain to come, and the courtyard nearly flooded.

On another occasion, the village chief called me into a mud hut where he and two elders gathered.

"Mamadou, we have been discussing your presence in the village—about why you are here."

"Oh, no!" I thought to myself. "This is where they kick me out running and screaming!"

"Mamadou," the village chief continued, "we want to plan well. We have decided we will have a delegation of elders that will travel from courtyard to courtyard to sign people up to become Christians."

"Uhhhh, is that right? Wow, that's great that you want to help. It doesn't quite work that way. But we can have more discussions about this later."

I was overjoyed. Over the last few years, I had been on a journey to leave behind a self-focused life. Jesus clearly sent me to live in a place where I was the "one Christian someone knew." He sent me to live among an ethnic group called the Wassoulou, who trace their history back 1,000 years and had no Christians, no churches, and no one trying to share with them the love of Jesus.[7] They were Muslims whose sorcery was feared throughout Mali. I lived in their midst, and people sought me out almost daily expressing interest in the message and Person inside of me. Despite the discomforts of immersion in another language, living without basic conveniences, and being treated as a super-wealthy person in one of the least developed corners of the world, mission work came easy. And I had never felt more purpose in my life. But purpose often comes with a price.

---

[1] Dr. and Mrs. Howard Taylor, *Spiritual Secret of Hudson Taylor* (New Kensington: Whitaker House, 1996) 133.

[2] *Ibid.*, 144.

[3] When one lives in a different culture, surprising cravings arise. I rarely drink sodas in America, but I craved Dr. Pepper in Mali. Since they were unavailable in the country, I bartered with missionaries in other countries to bring cases back home.

[4] One day, my truck broke down. We finally found a mechanic after a few days, but he was only experienced with motorcycles. He tinkered with my vehicle to make it functional enough to wobble several hours to a real mechanic.

[5] Malians are resourceful (e.g., chairs are made from recycled plastic bags, empty cans become "soccer balls," and Air France eye masks are used by motorcycle drivers as nose and mouth protection from dust and smog).

[6] Death was common in the village. After someone died, villagers rarely talked about it. "What did he die from?" I would ask. The standard reply was, "He just died. He's gone."

[7] At least, that we knew of.

8

Sumaya

So we do not lose heart. Though our outer self is wasting away, our inner self is being renewed day by day. For this light momentary affliction is preparing for us an eternal weight of glory beyond all comparison, as we look not to the things that are seen but to the things that are unseen. For the things that are seen are transient, but the things that are unseen are eternal (2 Corinthians 4:16-18).

THE PEOPLE OF MALI love proverbs—pithy and weighty statements that carry the wisdom of their ancestors. Everyone has heard that "a picture is worth a thousand words." In Mali, proverbs are worth more. I have heard lengthy arguments silenced when bearded old men interjected several-word bolts of wisdom. These proverbs disseminate the power, wisdom, and values of society. The most common response I hear to a Malian proverb is, "Ahhhh, now you see. There is nothing more to say."

There is a proverb I often use to make Malians burst into laughter—sometimes slapping each other in disbelief at my use of their language. The proverb relates to my desire—and struggle—in adapting to Malian culture. The dialogue often unfolds in the following way.

Malian: *"Ɛ, Mamadou, i bɛ an kan mɛn dɛ! I ye maliden yɛrɛ yɛre ye."* ("Eh, Mamadou, you really understand our language! You are a real Malian").

Me: *"Ne balimakɛ, i yɛrɛ b'a dɔn. Jirikurun mɛn o mɛn ji la, a tɛ kɛ bama ye."* ("My brother, you know this. No matter how long a log sits on the water, it can never become a crocodile").

The proverb means that no matter how much something resembles something else, it is, after all, different. No matter how hard I tried, how much Bambara I learned, or how much I dressed like a Malian. No matter how well I learned their customs, lived how they lived, ate what they ate, or drank what they drank, in the end, I would never become Malian. I would always be different.

After my several survey trips, I only had 10 days living among the Wassoulou before I returned to Bamako for a quick break. By that point, most of my dreams occurred in Bambara as I had not spoken a word of English. A year's worth of events seemed to happen in that short week and a half in Bandogo, and I needed to return to the city for a couple of days to process, rest, and grab supplies. That fact alone shows I was a log and not a crocodile.

Nevertheless, after two days in Bamako, I was anxious to return to Bandogo the next day. I intended to spend my final day in Bamako at Western-style restaurants with friends, but I was forced to stay inside with a fever and diarrhea. Such interruptions were common in Mali. Most American missionaries experienced frequent bouts of illness. Sickness became a part of our routine—a chance to catch up on reading, email, etc.

Even malaria, which terrifies the typical American, was common among our missionaries. I was one of the few on my team to evade malaria that first year in Mali, but we were all trained to combat the disease. For starters, we took our malaria prophylaxis—the best preventative option since malaria vaccines are still under development.[1] Mefloquine, also known as Lariam, was the drug of choice at the time because it was cheap and effective enough for long-term use. Despite the occasional hallucinatory dream (especially in the initial stages of taking the drug), Mefloquine's side effects were bearable for most people. If people were infected with malaria, they usually experienced chills and endured liquids coming out both ends for only a day or so. The experience was like a severe case of the flu for 24 hours. Since we had plenty of the prescribed drug on hand, we self-diagnosed if we experienced malaria symptoms and took the pills for treatment. After a day, one felt lethargic and sore from the puking and diarrhea, but by that time, the worst of a typical malaria bout had passed.

Since I only had a fever and diarrhea, I did not self-diagnose, but I visited the local clinic to check for malaria. The test came back negative, so we figured I had a virus that would soon end. After a few more days of diarrhea, an escalating fever, and the addition of vomiting, I dropped by one of the best clinics in the city. We checked again for malaria. Negative. The doctor told me the disease should pass. A couple of days later, however, I returned to the same doctor when my temperature exceeded 104 degrees Fahrenheit. They ran the malaria test again. This time, the doctor turned to me and told me the result.

"*Sumaya*. Malaria."

By that time, I could not swallow anything, even water, without an unwanted return on my deposit. I tried taking the pills for treatment to no avail. As a result, I stayed in a bed at the clinic for three days of intravenous quinine treatment.

Staying in a Malian clinic for treatment differed from an American hospital experience. No one stayed overnight. As a result, someone dropped me off at the clinic as soon as the doors opened. The nurses took me to a room to hook up my IV where I stayed until the clinic closed in the evening. The clinic also closed for mid-day Muslim prayers on Fridays. One of my teammates happened to be in the same clinic on a Friday receiving intravenous treatment for another disease. The building administrator left us hooked up to our IVs and kicked everyone else out to pray at the mosque. No one was in the clinic but us!

The Weakness

Dr. Guindo at the medical clinic was the doctor of choice for many expats and wealthy Malians. He had decades of experience diagnosing and treating people infected with malaria. He later told me I had the second-worst case of malaria he had ever seen for someone taking a prophylaxis.

I did not ask him about the worst.

But he made my mind race back to Bandogo where mosquitoes sucked on my body like candy. I wore thong sandals, and even though I used bug repellent, I had over 50 mosquito bites on my feet and lower legs. I slept with a mosquito net, but I sometimes woke to discover a mosquito sucking on my leg or arm through the net. I killed them right away, but dead mosquitos with splattered blood decorated my hut.

Once one is infected, malaria's symptoms take around five days to commence. I had begun feeling some of those effects when I returned to Bamako, but the malaria tests came back negative—which occurred, we later discovered, because my prophylaxis skewed the results. Since we did not immediately treat for malaria, we gave malaria more time to wreak havoc. By the time we began treatment, my body was in a worse condition than any of us imagined.

After I had awakened from sleep following the third day of quinine treatment, diarrhea and vomiting had ceased, but something new and frightening had taken over my body. When I tried to rise from bed, my legs wobbled like Jell-O, and I couldn't stand. I managed to reach the phone to call for help, but not without a disjointed, crippled hobble that resembled a severe case of multiple sclerosis, myasthenia gravis, or polio.

I was afraid. Malaria did not scare me. We knew about malaria's effects and how to take care of the disease. But no one knew what was happening to me. My weakness befuddled Dr. Guindo. "These are not symptoms of malaria or your prophylaxis," he claimed. "I have no idea what is happening."

We called an American doctor friend who was a tropical disease specialist. He came to see me at home. "Fascinating," he said. "It looks like you have a virus. I don't think the disease is life-threatening, but I am not sure what is happening."

There were no other doctors worth visiting. In the meantime, I only improved gradually. I rested and barely moved for three days. My reward was the ability to walk 100 yards without a crippled gait, only to have the weakness return. This pattern continued for two weeks. During that period, I also came down with other diseases. My immune system was working overtime.

That third week, our missionary team had a trip planned to Dogon country up north—a two days' drive from Bamako. My team did not know what to do with me. All the people who took care of me planned to be on the trip. At the same time, I showed signs of improvement in the days leading up to the trek—even enduring full days without weakness. My supervisors decided to take me as long as I refrained from strenuous activity.

Even though I was robbed of returning to Bandogo when desired, I was excited to spend time with teammates in a fascinating area of the country.[2] Although still weak, I joined a couple of short hikes—mostly without a limp. Toward the end of our trip, however, I came down with chills. Then diarrhea. Then vomiting. *Sumaya* had struck again.[3] And we were a day's drive away from a hospital.

My body was under attack. Reality sunk in that I was experiencing another bout of malaria. I lay on the couch with my knees propped up, head tilted back, and my eyes closed as teammates prayed for my healing. As they prayed, however, I thought less about my healing and more about the Wassoulou.

An image entered my mind. Satan was attacking me with sickness, trying to discourage me, dissuade me, and destroy me to keep me away from the Wassoulou. Satan waged war against me as I dared to bring the light of Jesus to a place that had been his realm for so long. I saw myself, standing alone between the Wassoulou and the presence of God. The fire of war raged around me. I looked toward God with a steely determination in my eyes, resolving to stand before him on behalf of the Wassoulou—no matter what that took or what was thrown at me.

As the image faded and my teammates continued to pray, my nose scrunched up, I gritted my teeth, and I began saying with determination, "I. Will. Not. Give. Up."

"I. Will. Not. Give. Up."

And, finally, I screamed.

"I. WILL. NOT. GIVE. UP!!!!"

Losing the Battle

I took the malaria treatment that evening, and we headed back to Bamako the next morning. I needed nutrients and to stay hydrated but everything I ate or drank gushed through my body.

Restrooms were scarce on the return journey. At one point, we stopped at a gas station restroom, which utilized the typical Malian "squatty potty" instead of a toilet. The restroom was comfortably enclosed in a building and included a porcelain area to place one's feet around the targeted hole. Normally, such arrangements were fine, but my weakness was fierce. I had trouble standing. Squatting seemed impossible. Malaria ran through my blood. I vomited and had diarrhea simultaneously. My leg strength had vanished, but I strained to remain squatting to dispose of my waste cleanly. I was in misery—to the point of sad, pitiful tears. Flies swarmed up from the latrine, and I even sat on the latrine's hole for a moment, succumbing to my leg's weakness. I felt low. Disgusting. Filthy. Pathetic. Less than human. And as if my body was spinning out of control.

We returned to Bamako, and my extreme weakness came and went for the next few days. One evening, however, as around 10 of our teammates ate dinner together, I zoned in and out—my body fighting the weakness. I excused myself from the dinner table and hobbled to a chair hoping to escape the weakness with sleep. Four weeks had passed since I first came down with malaria, and I was just getting over the second bout.

Then, all of a sudden, my body began twitching, and I gasped for air. Kathy, one of my supervisors and a nurse, rushed over to me. Teammates surrounded me.

"What's wrong? What's wrong?" they cried.

"Having. Trouble. Breathing." I managed to utter.

My body convulsed some more as I continued to struggle breathing. I heard the cries of my teammates.

"What's happening?!!? What's happening?!?!"

My body went into a seizure—which I had never experienced. I couldn't stop shaking.

"You're panicking! You're panicking! Breathe slowly!" I heard Kathy say.

But I had no control. Then, as suddenly as the seizure began, I stopped breathing.

---

[1] A friend who worked in Niger while I was in Mali died of malaria. I am not sure if he was taking his prophylaxis, but he could not stay hydrated enough while fighting the disease in the African bush. His death alarmed us.

[2] The Dogon are one of the most studied people groups in Africa. Fleeing Islamization up to 1,000 years ago, they migrated hundreds of miles to live as cliff-dwellers in an area easy to defend. Although they eventually succumbed to the influence of Islam, they retain a significant amount of their animistic heritage which they display with colorful dances, masks, and carved wooden doors that tell their myths.

[3] Relapses of malaria can occur even decades after an initial infection.

purple heart 9

NOT LONG AGO, MY wife Nichole and I watched a movie entitled *Mary and Martha.*[1] The movie tells the story of two women who overcome grief by combating malaria in Africa. As I watched child after child die in the movie, I realized I had never actually seen someone die from malaria. Before the children died, they all had uncontrollable seizures and gasped for breath.

I was shaken.

Nichole looked at me. "Are you okay? Do I need to turn it off?"

I was in tears. I am not a doctor, and I cannot explain what happened to me the day I went into a seizure in Mali, but what I experienced seemed to be what those children in the movie experienced the moment before they died.

I was overwhelmed with emotion from what happened to me over a decade ago. The memories flooded back fresh and raw. I felt the nervous energy and thankfulness for life that comes from a brush with death—like I did one day in Bamako when an out-of-control vehicle careened onto the shoulder and brushed against my shirt going 50 miles an hour.[2] Surreal shock. Life can end in an instant. I took a deep breath and reminded myself, "I'm alive."

I'm not sure how long I was unable to breathe that day in Mali. Maybe only a few seconds. But when I lost my ability to breathe, my body's convulsions intensified.

Then, as quickly as my body had lost control, the seizure stopped, my windpipes opened, and I breathed. I froze in shock for a moment. Then, my eyes darted around the room in disbelief at what had happened.

My supervisors had seen enough. They began making arrangements to medevac me. Given a choice to fly to South Africa for medical attention (where I knew no one) or home to Texas, I chose home. Perhaps I did not make the best medical choice, but I was not thinking about the tropical disease expertise of doctors in Texas compared to those in South Africa. I wanted to recover near family. Looking back, however, I can see how God used this choice in his Superplan.

I was medically evacuated the next day. A medevac to America did not mean a private jet rushed me off to safety, but I did receive special attention getting on and off the plane. I traveled in first class (the only time I had done that!) and breezed past customs as assistants guided my wheelchair to the front of the line. Medevacs had perks!

Elusive Diagnosis

When I returned to Texas a month after contracting malaria, I could only walk with an awkward limp for minutes at a time, and my voice sounded like someone gasping for water in the desert. I heard later that an old high school coach, upon describing my appearance to a friend, said, "He looked like death. I saw death in his eyes."

My parents rushed me to the emergency room. The doctors determined I was malnourished and gave me nutrition packs intravenously. Even though I ate regularly and drank plenty of fluids over the next two weeks, I was forced to return to the ER for treatment. Nutrients slipped through my digestive system like it was a water slide.

In search of a diagnosis and treatment, I started off visiting infectious disease doctors. They shipped a dozen vials of my blood to laboratories to check for short-term curable diseases. Within days, all the results came back negative.

Then, they shipped off vials of blood checking for long-term incurable diseases such as myasthenia gravis.[3]

I spent most of those first weeks in Texas on my parents' recliner. Only a few weeks prior, I had been living in Bandogo, alive with purpose and feeling the pleasure of God while fulfilling his plan of being "the one Christian someone knows." My journey to Bandogo was full of counter-cultural decisions—choosing God's Superplan instead of my own or that of others. From the outside, those choices seemed detrimental as my body's outline formed on my parents' recliner while I often stared at nothing in particular without the energy even to watch TV. I hoped someone would tell me if I was going to die or not, or if I would walk and function normally again. God had a plan, however, when I couldn't see beyond my daily survival.

Sometimes there are dark places in God's Superplan, when our hope is frail, and we fail to see what God is doing. After all, Jesus cried out before his impending crucifixion, "My soul is crushed with grief to the point of death," and, "My Father! If it is possible, let this cup of suffering be taken away from me. Yet I want your will to be done, not mine."[4]

The perk of having a handicapped-parking sticker wore off quickly. A diagnosis of a long-term incurable disease felt more desirable than continuing in uncertainty. The thought seems ridiculous now, but even knowing I would die seemed more comforting than the unknown. What my life was, or would be, remained in limbo. And we could do nothing but wait and pray.

The day came when the infectious disease doctors gave the incurable disease results.

"Negative. We have no idea what's happening with you. We're going to send you to a neurologist to check for muscle or nerve damage."

Off I went to Dr. Payne—that was his name if I remember correctly. Or maybe I only remember my experience with him, which I likened to an imaginary movie where a doctor—Dr. Pain—uses his practice to torture people. He did an electromyography (EMG) all over my body. The process involved inserting electrode needles into my muscles and administering electric shocks through the needles to check for muscle damage. Then, to check for nerve damage, electrodes were taped to my skin as the doctor measured the speed and strength of electric signals between multiple points. I was like an electric pincushion.

I usually have a high tolerance for pain. I had even played a year of college tennis with shoulder, elbow, and wrist injuries that required weekly electric shock treatments. But for some reason, what I experienced with Dr. Pain felt like barbaric torture. Most electric shocks caused my body to twitch. Every time my body twitched the machine did not read properly, necessitating another shock in the same place. Every time I was shocked again in the same place, that part of my body became more sensitive to the shock, which caused more pain and twitching. Every time I felt more pain and twitching, my body sweated more. Because of the sweat, the electric shock inflicted more pain. It was a cascading horror.

I remember thinking that God taking my life would be much more preferable than experiencing that agony again. Dr. Pain did the most thorough job he could (he hooked me up to his torture chair for a couple of hours), but he released me early.

"Wow, I haven't tortured anyone like that in a long time," he said. "I don't see any muscle or nerve damage. I don't know what's happening to you."

By that point, the doctors told me there was no one left to see. "You can go see such-and-such doctor," they said, "but I doubt it will help." Almost three months had passed since malaria struck, and after my experience with Dr. Pain, I was not excited about more torture tests to check for long-shot possibilities, so I stopped seeing doctors. I knew people were praying for me around the world. If I was going to be healed, the healing would happen through the powerful hand of God.

Intimate with Weakness
Despite my weakness, painful shock tests, and fear of the unknown—or because of those trials—God was speaking to me. My prayers began by asking for release and healing, to return to physical comfort and normalcy. Even though I and others prayed, I was not healed.

I identified with a letter from Paul in ways that I previously could not relate. In 2 Corinthians 12:7-10, Paul mentions a "thorn in his flesh" that kept him from acting conceited. He asked for the thorn's removal three times, but God told Paul, "My grace is sufficient for you, for my power is made perfect in weakness." Paul then speaks of boasting in weakness so that Christ's power could be appropriated, and he exhorts the reader to be content in weakness, hardship, and calamity. "For when I am weak," he says, "then I am strong."

I began looking at my weakness and suffering in a different way. As a result of my American heritage, where safety and security are virtues and rights (not privileges), I viewed suffering as a condition to avoid or, at least, be prayed out of. There are times for such thoughts and prayers. But as I dove into "suffering" passages in the Bible, the Word of God formed a different response in me. Those in God's Superplan embraced suffering –even rejoiced in suffering—in ways I had never been challenged to employ.

"We rejoice in our sufferings," Paul said to the church in Rome, "knowing that suffering produces endurance, and endurance produces character, and character produces hope, and hope does not put us to shame, because God's love has been poured into our hearts" (Romans 5:3-5).

Rejoicing in suffering struck me as the proper response of Christ followers. When Peter and John experienced prison in Jerusalem and threats from those in power, they did not shrink back and pray for security and comfort. They prayed, "Lord, look upon their threats and grant to your servants to continue to speak your word with all boldness, while you stretch out your hand to heal, and signs and wonders are performed through the name of your holy servant Jesus" (Acts 4:29-30).

They prayed for God to work in power in the midst of trials. They prayed for boldness in the midst of suffering—not release. As a result, they "filled Jerusalem"[5] with the teaching of Jesus instead of obeying admonitions to be silent. The authorities wanted them killed, but eventually settled on warning and flogging them. With increased suffering, one might think the apostles would temper their response. Instead, they left their persecutors "rejoicing that they were counted worthy to suffer dishonor for the name. And every day, in the temple and from house to house, they did not cease teaching and preaching that the Christ is Jesus" (Acts 5:41-42).

No wonder I have heard about the Chinese church saying to American Christians, "Stop praying for persecution in China to end, for it is through persecution that the church has grown. In fact, we are praying that the American church might taste the same persecution, so revival would come to the American church like we have seen in China."[6]

The weakness in my body and my unknown illness became the "thorn in my flesh." I did not experience the more severe trials of physical or social persecution, but I became intimate with weakness, learning to embrace and rejoice in my suffering for the cause of Christ.

I realized the severity of my pride and independence, to the point where I had felt as if I did not need anyone else. Through my weakness, I needed people in a new way. Moreover, I needed God in ways I had never experienced. Without Christ, I was just a college graduate who spent most days on my parents' recliner.

When I had energy during those first few months of sickness, an outlet I used to process what I was going through was writing and recording songs. I bought the cheapest digital recorder I could find on eBay and recorded 15 songs. The chorus of the title track, "Out of Then," reflects some of the despair and raw emotions I felt at the time.

He's a hero,

Helpless in his state,

He's got a purple heart to wear without nothin' to share,

'Cause his heart's fade of color and bare.[7]

I had been fulfilling my calling—my dream. I had pictured myself living in Africa the rest of my life. But I was like a soldier who had trained for war only to be shipped home after taking a bullet in the first battle. I felt as if I had a purple heart in God's mission. People encouraged me about the sacrifice I had made for God. They talked of my noble cause and prayed for my healing. But all I thought about was leaving the battle early.

If there was ever a season to return to a life focused on my own path and plans, and merely inviting God into them, that was the time. People heralded my efforts and would welcome me back to normalcy. I could even pat myself on the back for having experienced the front lines of pioneer missions. I felt the gravitational pull of America to abandon the radical way of Jesus. I felt as if I could go back and everyone would embrace my decision. I heard their voices,

"You need to take care of yourself now."

"Don't be rogue."

"That wasn't God's plan if you came back like this."

"Maybe you weren't hearing God's will correctly."

"You've paid your dues."

"You're being careless and not thinking about others."

"There are plenty of ministry opportunities right here."

While my body struggled for strength and my mind dealt with uncertainty, the greatest battle for me at that time was an unseen, spiritual crossroads. Would I return to a life defined by personal preferences and the expectations of others, especially in light of my current consequences for not doing so? Sometimes following God's Superplan involves pressing forward in faith when doing so seems like madness to others. Hebrews 11:1 says, "Faith is the assurance of things hoped for, the conviction of things not seen." In the same chapter, people like Abraham are described as those who "died in faith, not having received the things promised, but having seen them and greeted them from afar, and having acknowledged that they were strangers and exiles on the earth."[8] Living in God's Superplan involves a disposition of faith as one who embraces the identity of a stranger and exile on earth as part of God's Kingdom.

I remember not being able to pray in ways I was accustomed. I did not have the energy or ability to concentrate for long periods. After nearly four months of illness, however, I distinctly remember a strange prayer I prayed. It was non-verbal, more of a symbolic image. I felt the battle of whether or not to stick with the call God had placed on my life—of whether or not that call had changed due to my illness. In my prayer, my hand ascended and grasped for

God—feeble, but willing and able. "There is no other way," my hand symbolized. "I cannot abandon your path, God. I will serve you, no matter what that means."

Coincidence or not, shortly after that prayer, my strength improved. I began seeing a physical therapist. In my early twenties, I fought for strength and mobility alongside gray-haired people recovering from strokes. Within a week or two, I could walk without a limp again. Although still experiencing chronic diarrhea and fatigue, I could walk into a room again without eliciting a gaze from others that reflected my wretched state.

Half-Dead Recruiter

Ironically, even though half-dead and failed as an overseas missionary, my mission organization asked me to be a mobilizer—a recruiter—to find more missionaries to send to West Africa. I agreed to do so, as long as they understood I needed to rest after each trip because of my diminished strength. I was excited to visit churches, schools, and mission conferences to share stories and challenge Christians to be on mission with God.

One of my first trips was to a missions conference at Toccoa Falls College—a small, Christian school in northeast Georgia. Upon arrival, I met the conference coordinator, a recent graduate named Nichole Gruber. I remember Nichole's smile and outstretched hand as she walked across the room to meet me, and that she was not only beautiful, but also wearing a red West African dress. I was instantly attracted to her. An hour later, I heard she was in final preparations for moving to West Africa as a career missionary.

I was smitten. And we began a relationship that eventually led to our marriage.

Nichole was not the only person I recruited. God used me to call three people straight out of college to work among the Wassoulou and the people of Bandogo. I knew God called them because there was no way that I, a half-dead, crippled recruiter, could have convinced anyone to leave everything and live in the same place where my suffering originated.

Everything seemed to be falling into place. My sickness and medical evacuation were resulting in more workers among the Wassoulou. Even my former supervisors planned on becoming long-term missionaries among the Wassoulou, even though they would not begin until six months after the arrival of the other three recruits.

In the meantime, I could not stop thinking about returning to Bandogo. Besides, who would train and orient those three new missionaries? I had not left Mali willingly, and I never felt released from the work. A resolve built up in me that my involvement was not complete. I prayed daily for the first Wassoulou churches to start, and I felt the urgency of openness in Bandogo and the surrounding villages. I had picked up knowledge of the language and culture. I was passionate about the opportunity and willing to go. And I could finally walk again. I couldn't stay in America.

When I asked my mission board about returning to Mali, they replied that people with my missionary status (i.e., lowly) are not allowed to return after being medevacked, but they would inquire with leadership. I pleaded with them to let me return, offering to pay my expenses.[9] They later replied and agreed to purchase my round-trip airfare to match my presence in Mali with the arrival of the new missionaries.

Getting Healthy

My life had changed dramatically in the nine months since contracting malaria. In the midst of being removed from the Wassoulou and facing an uncertain future with sickness, God was speaking to me about a number of issues. I was too comfortable working on my own. God was chipping away at my pride. In a healthy way, I started needing people and needing God. Without such change, I would have never been ready for, among other things, a relationship with Nichole.

Furthermore, I started paying more attention to my health. Although properly motivated, my attempts "to go native" in Bandogo were reckless. I drank and ate everything so as not to offend, but my Malian friends would have understood if I had explained my stomach was American and not Malian!

Modeled after Jesus who incarnated himself into a particular culture (first-century Jewish) to point to God's Kingdom, I had sought to be an incarnational witness in Bandogo. But I started rethinking this approach. In Bandogo, I had attempted to throw away all aspects of my culture to communicate as pure a gospel message as possible. There is no way as an American, however, that I could fully incarnate the gospel in another culture. I could make attempts, but the gospel could only take root in a culture when many people from that society gave their lives to Jesus and interpreted and lived out the Scripture in their own context.

I had felt guilty for having possessions. I feared I would distance myself from the Wassoulou for being from a country of opportunity, so I had tried to act as if I had no access to that privilege. That posture was disingenuous. Long-term, for my emotional, physical, and spiritual health, I needed to be honest with myself and others about my identity—which was influenced by my culture—while still seeking to communicate and live out a clear message of Jesus to people from a different culture. In wrestling with this topic, Jonathan Bonk, a seasoned missions scholar later advised me:

> *Most missionaries from the economically advantaged parts of the world must accept and learn to play the role of "righteous rich" as defined contextually but deeply informed biblically. [Western missionaries] can be useful to these people, on their terms, and on the Bible's terms, in contextually appropriate ways that will enable [the missionaries] to maintain [their] integrity and [their] cultural identity (American), and a culturally appropriate, recognized and appreciated role ("Our rich person").*[10]

It might be true that a log cannot become a crocodile. But if a log knows it's a log, identifies as such, lives in the same place as crocodiles, and happens to scare others because of the resemblance, that is another matter.

When I began walking normally again, I assumed my other health problems would quickly subside. Instead, almost a year after first contracting malaria, I still experienced chronic diarrhea and fatigue. Hearing of my health problems, numerous people offered their advice.

"I have a cousin who had a weird disease. He started taking large doses of such-and-such supplement and was healed. You should do the same."

"America doesn't want people to know this because it would kill pharmaceutical companies, but if you just…"

"You know, there's a guy across the border in Mexico. It's illegal in the U.S., but…"

I have heard it all.

One particular nutritionist, Dr. Luepnitz, was frequently recommended to me. At first, like most medical advice I received, I ignored the recommendations.

"Nutritionists are quacks," I presumed. "Besides, the name Luepnitz sounds strangely similar to 'loopy.'"

Despite my reservations, I knew my physical condition needed to improve before I could return to Mali. Nine months of chronic diarrhea and fatigue did not bode well for a return to the village! Without showing improvement through other means, I was desperate enough to visit the nutritionist. It helped that my friends who recommended him said he worked with Olympic athletes and was a devout Christian.

Because every doctor I had seen had the same clueless remarks about my symptoms, I expected the same result with the nutritionist, but he surprised me.

Dr. Luepnitz showed particular interest in meeting me after my friends told him my story. He asked me to send him all my medical reports, including the ones in French, to review before my visit. By that point, I had collected hundreds of pages of medical records.

I sat down in his office 11 months after my initial bout of malaria. He gave a curious smile as I retold the events and symptoms of my sickness. Instead of the familiar puzzled look, Dr. Luepnitz frequently nodded as if he already knew what I was going to say next. He held his smile after I completed my story. Then he spoke.

"I know what happened to you."

Coming off a year of visiting bewildered doctors, I initially thought his words sounded ridiculous. But then he continued, with half of what he said going over my head and half retained. I could tell he was a genius who cared about me and my mission work. He gave me the following explanation, trying to speak down to my level:

I have been praying for you the last few weeks. Ever since I received your medical records, I have been poring over them asking help from God to heal you. I had all your medical records in French translated into English. I know what happened to you.

Your body fought malaria so hard that your immune system was shot. Then, you picked up other diseases—so many, that no medical test could isolate one disease, which is why the tests returned negative. You can see from this test that your blood cell counts are astronomically high. Your body has exhausted the use of trained blood cells and has resorted to using untrained ones to fight disease. Your gastric lining is destroyed and, even though you eat normally, most nutrients pass through your body without being used.

Because you were fighting disease so hard and not able to retain nutrients as needed, such as proteins, your body has been cannibalizing itself—like what happens with severely anorexic people. Your body has been stripping proteins from your major muscle groups in your upper legs and arms to keep your heart beating. And, you are close to needing a full blood transfusion.

You are lucky to be alive. The Lord must have a reason for that.

I vacillated between slumping in my chair and jumping out of it. On the one hand, I felt the severity of my condition. On the other hand, someone finally gave me an explanation! Then, Dr. Luepnitz uttered words that felt both absurd and like fresh water.

"I know what to do to get you back to health. Take these supplements to repair your digestive system and restore your strength. Go on this high-protein, right-carb diet. Within three weeks, you should have normal stools again and a noticeable return of strength."

"That's it?!" I thought to myself. "It's that simple?" I was doubtful, but he was brilliant, confident, and caring, and I could not help but follow and trust his instruction.

"So," I asked, "what are your thoughts about me returning to Mali for six months—leaving in four weeks?"

He gave me the purely health-conscious answer—which was an obvious, "No." Then, he gave me the Christian mentor and nutritionally informed answer, which was a hesitant, "Yes." He was confident my health would soon improve, and he would load me with supplements to help combat the disease-ridden world of Mali.

We prayed together. And Dr. Luepnitz refused payment.

Within three weeks, I had a noticeable return of strength and normal stools, which felt great after a year of not having them! I celebrated by hiking part of the Appalachian Trail. Four weeks after seeing Dr. Luepnitz, feeling like a new man, I boarded an Air France plane to Mali, confident, excited, thankful, strengthened, and feeling destined to see the Lord accomplish in the next six months what I was taken away from the year before.

---

[1] *Mary and Martha*, Dir. Phillip Noyce, Working Title Television, 2013, Film.

[2] That event occurred after Mali won a crucial match in the 2002 African Nations Cup. While walking home on the shoulder of the main road, a public transport vehicle full of celebrating Malians (drunk maybe?) careened onto the shoulder toward myself and three Malian men. As we jumped out of the way, I felt the vehicle touch my loose shirt. Later, we heard that several people died on the road during the post-match "celebration."

[3] A long-term neuromuscular disease that leads to varying degrees of skeletal muscle weakness.

[4] Matthew 26:38-39 New Living Translation.

[5] Acts 5:28.

[6] Jimmy Draper, "Call to Prayer: Persecution from a Chinese Christian's Perspective," *Baptist Press*, 30 May 2014, www.bpnews.net/42677/call-to-prayer-persecution-from-a-chinese-christians-perspective, Accessed 23 Mar. 2017.

[7] You can listen to the song at https://soundcloud.com/clayman-chris/04-out-of-then.

[8] Hebrews 11:13.

[9] Round-trip tickets to Mali range from $1,200-$2,300.

[10] Jonathan Bonk, Message to Chris Clayman, 17 May 2005, Email.

10

return

*Is anyone among you sick? Let him call for the elders of the
church, and let them pray over him, anointing him with oil
in the name of the Lord. And the prayer of faith will save the
one who is sick, and the Lord will raise him up. And if he
has committed sins, he will be forgiven (James 5:14-15).*

I STEPPED OUT OF the plane in Bamako, Mali one year after my initial bout of malaria. The air was dusty and hot—and beautiful.
It is surprising what one embraces after having it taken away. A
welcoming party awaited me at the airport: teammates and friends,
as well as a stranger visiting Mali on a volunteer trip.

The stranger said, "I came across your newsletters from the last
two years on a church's website, and I have been following your journey. I had to be at the airport to see your face when you returned."

My face was full of anticipation, delight, and redemption. My
face smiled as if I was returning home.

I fought jet lag for a day or two, then headed to Bandogo. What
pleasure it was to be in my village again, apologizing and explaining
my absence in person, catching up on the last year of activity (including the unexpected deaths in the village), and laughing together
over sweet, potent tea.

One woman I did not recognize approached me with a toddler
in her arms. She handed me the child and said, "This is your child.
Mamadou, this is your child."

I looked around in confusion. I might be ignorant about many
subjects, but I knew how babies were made, and there was no way
I had a child.

"Mamadou," the village chief's older brother intervened, "she means that this child would not exist without you. Do you remember the time you brought the American doctors to our village to help us?"

"Yes."

"This child was going to die. But those doctors kept the baby alive. And you brought the doctors here. This is your child."

Actually, others were mainly responsible for the American doctors coming, but there was no point in arguing. I helped lead that trip, and the grateful mother's point was taken. I prayed a blessing over the mother and child, returned the toddler, and soaked in the fulfillment of my reunion with Bandogo.

The village chief and elders, while troubled over my sickness, expressed excitement about my return. When I broached the subject of three more North Americans living in the village, they extended their welcome.

In addition, a friend from college agreed to accompany me for the duration of my stay in Mali. As Jesus sent out his disciples two-by-two to different villages, we planned to follow the same pattern, carrying few possessions, visiting as many Wassoulou villages as possible throughout Mali, Guinea, and Cote d'Ivoire, and staying where we found houses of peace.[1] We were excited to discover where God was at work to assist the new missionaries in spreading the hope of Jesus to new villages.

Shocked and Shaken

My stay in Bandogo was cut short by a required conference in Senegal, which started one week after I arrived in Mali. On one of the first days at the conference, I noticed blood in my stool. I inquired with a missionary doctor on site, and he diagnosed me with amoebic dysentery. I took the treatment and felt weak for a few days, but the weakness was mild compared to what I had been through the previous year.

After one week in Senegal, I returned to Mali feeling healthy and excited about my next adventure to Wassoulou land. But then, a thief snuck in and stole my dream. I woke up in the middle of the night sweating profusely and shivering with chills. My head pulsed with fever. I sat up and immediately knew what was happening—*sumaya*.

I was paralyzed with shock—more so at God than the sickness. "How could this happen?" I felt certain that God wanted me to return to Mali for those few months. More at that point than any in my life, I felt a crisis of faith. How could I be so confident about God leading me to Mali and become so sick again? I was shocked, bewildered, and shaken—and I knew that another medevac awaited.

My bed was only 20 feet from the kitchen cabinet that stored my malaria pills for treatment, but my sickness and dizziness complicated the trek. I stumbled down the hall as if in a drunken stupor, opened the kitchen cabinet, and swiped at the medicine bottle before falling to the ground. The bottle crashed, scattering pills in every direction. With my body sprawled on the kitchen floor, I scraped up a few pills, swallowed, closed my eyes, and questioned God.

"Why?!"

Days later, when talking to a supervisor, I said I felt humiliated.

"You mean humbled," she said.

"No, I mean humiliated."

I was so confident I was supposed to be in Mali for six months, but I was forced to leave within a month, without even getting started! Again! Two weeks after contracting malaria, my supervisors agreed I needed to return to the States. I took a quick trip to Wassoulou land to say good-bye. I felt like Moses. I had wandered through the desert to reach my destination, but God did not allow me to enter. Parting conversations with the village chief and others were sad and tinged with thoughts of what could have been. I knew a return was unlikely. Then, disgracefully, I was medevacked to Texas for the second time in a year.

Over the next few months, not only did my former supervisors back out of becoming missionaries among the Wassoulou, but also the three people I recruited struggled with life in the village. A year passed before they could last more than a few days in Bandogo without returning early to Bamako due to sickness, nervous breakdowns, or other trauma. My friend from college lasted only a month or two in Mali before departing due to the hardship. What was fitting together so perfectly seemed crumbled and failed. In God's Superplan, the outcome sometimes looks bleak.

Moving On

As part of her undergraduate degree, Nichole had studied and written a thesis about the Maninka people of West Africa. I had visited Maninka villages in which the people risked their lives in man-made holes in search of gold. I knew God was leading Nichole and me toward marriage. Preparing to ask her to marry me, I bought "Maninka" gold and had a ring fashioned for her with the following inscription:

Ala k'an ka sumunta mɛn.

When I asked the gold salesman if he could inscribe this Bambara proverb on the ring, he told me to repeat the proverb over and over. He had no idea what I was saying. An old man chuckled in the corner. "Eh, city boy, this white man speaks better Bambara than you. All you young people are losing our language. You don't know this proverb?!"

The proverb is an ancient one spoken to newly married couples. The literal translation in English is, "May God make our campfire last." The meaning, as explained to me, is that in the traditional Malian village, the day was full of activities—cooking, farming, cleaning, etc. The husband and wife rarely saw each other during the day. If a marriage was strong and lasting, however, the man and woman talked over a fire late into the night. Therefore, a common wedding blessing was, "May God make our night fire—or campfire—last a long time."

When I returned from Mali, Nichole and I made preparations for marriage. During that process, however, we realized we had both met as individuals who felt called to live the rest of our lives in Africa. Due to my health issues, my future in Africa was, at best, uncertain. Through our conversations and prayer, God matured our understanding of his calling.

God showed us that we were to get married. As much as we felt called to Africa, we were called even more to the journey with God. And he wanted us to take that journey together, wherever that led. Our callings to specific places and ministries can become like boxes in which we try to contain God. He calls us to specific places and ministries at times, but we have to be willing to ask God what he desires and allow him to redirect our calling. The call is to the relational journey with God.

We were married a few months after my second medevac, and I started seminary in Texas the following month. My ongoing struggle with illness kept me from working, but Nichole worked to provide for our family. Two years after our wedding, Nichole gave birth to our first child, a son. We had no idea what the future held, but we knew our family remained on God's path.

Ongoing Weakness

Based on my prior experience, I avoided other doctors and went straight to Dr. Luepnitz after my second medevac. He was shocked to hear what had happened. He gave advice on how I could return to health, which consisted of more supplements and a particular diet, and I followed his orders.

Unfortunately, the nutritional approach alone did not overcome my weakness the second time around. Besides recurring fatigue and diarrhea, I had a strange new demonstration of weakness. Around three or four times a day, my arms and hands curled up, my neck slouched down, and I quivered in weakness for 10 minutes or so. I was so weak that I often curled into a ball and waited for the episode to end. The weak spells usually occurred after trying to bend over, going two hours without food, or standing too long. Running, picking up large objects, and other strenuous physical activities were out of the question. While I could walk normally on most occasions, at times, I was so weak that my multiple sclerosis-like gait returned.

I repeated the infectious disease protocol.

"Fascinating," the doctors said. "I don't think you are in danger of dying, but we have no idea what is happening."

Desperate for answers, we spent a full week at the Mayo Clinic in Minnesota, which has a reputation for diagnosing and treating rare diseases. I was impressed by their integrated health approach in which doctors from different disciplines worked together to help patients. Nevertheless, after the week ended, the response was the same.

"Fascinating, we don't know what is happening."

My weak spells continued for two and a half years after my second evacuation from Mali. In total, I battled debilitating illness or weakness for three and a half years.

I tried to function normally, but my strength severely limited me. Nichole and I attempted to start ministry among Somali and Kurdish refugees in apartment complexes. We established solid relationships with families, but my health could not keep up, and we backed out. I kept a light seminary schedule, read and wrote for my classes, attended church meetings, and spent quality time with Nichole.

I often sat in a room of socializing church members, watching them move effortlessly and talk with vibrancy as I battled a weak spell in the corner. I was "that guy" in the room—the one I assume new people had to ask others in hushed tones, "What's wrong with him?" I had no idea what would become of me, if I would ever function normally again. I came to view my weakness and digestive issues as the "new normal." Nichole and I continued to pray, to prepare, and to plod, but we had no idea what lay ahead when I finished seminary.

Where Can We Go?

James 5:14-15 says, "Is anyone among you sick? Let him call for the elders of the church, and let them pray over him, anointing him with oil in the name of the Lord. And the prayer of faith will save the one who is sick, and the Lord will raise him up."

Shortly after my first medevac from Mali, I sat in a Sunday service at a large church when those verses came to mind. I felt prodded to walk forward at the end of the service to ask for the elders to pray for my healing. But I realized, in all my years of attending similar churches, I had never seen these verses applied. I was afraid that presenting such a request in the church service would make the leaders uncomfortable and create a spectacle. Perhaps the discomfort was solely mine, but I did not go forward that day. "Besides," I thought, "people are praying for me all over the world."

Three years later, I was battling ongoing weak spells and an impending graduation from seminary the next spring when Nichole brought these verses to mind. Even though people had continued praying for me, there is something more active, demonstrative, and humbling to submit oneself to elders in the faith, calling for them to pray for healing. I gathered with leaders from the seminary. They anointed me with oil and faithfully prayed for my healing. I met with the elders of my church. They did the same.

Coincidence or not, after two and a half years of weakness following my second medevac, I stopped having weak spells shortly after these prayers were prayed. I have not had one since.

With my body on the mend and the end of seminary in sight, Nichole and I began to dream about the future. We knew we couldn't immediately live in Africa. My health was not nearly as robust as the first time I had attempted to return to Mali, and that had not gone well.

We discovered a job request from my previous mission board for a couple to start churches among Malians in Paris. The job description fit perfectly. We could work with Malian Muslims, learn French, and live in a country without malaria. The mission board could send missionaries with experience in West Africa, one of whom spoke Bambara. Win-win! I talked to the leaders in Paris. They showed immense interest but stressed they could not reserve the position until we received medical approval.

We started the application process. A new medical doctor had begun working with the mission board, and one of his first cases was whether or not to accept us for service. The process took several months, but he finally approved us to work in countries without malaria. By that time, we were disheartened to learn that other people had filled the position in Paris. Despite our background and calling, the mission board said they couldn't send us to France.

Even though I still prayed every day for the first Wassoulou churches to start, working with Malians overseas did not seem possible. As a result, Nichole and I prayed about moving to Japan or China. Going to a place like Japan was intriguing because of my missionary call that came through Japanese friends. China was of interest because, unbeknownst to many, it is home to millions of Muslims. So, we prepared for a move to East Asia. After a couple of years, if my health improved, we figured we could attempt to live in West Africa again.

But then, a miraculous meeting changed everything.

---

[1] See Matthew 10:5-15 and Luke 10:1-12.

musa

*Brother will deliver brother over to death, and the
father his child, and children will rise against parents
and have them put to death, and you will be hated
by all for my name's sake. But the one who endures
to the end will be saved (Matthew 10:21-22).*

WHILE NICHOLE AND I weighed our ministry options, a friend contacted me saying he had moved to New York City to lead a church-planting initiative. He said there were many West Africans in Harlem and the Bronx and asked if I had ideas on how to start churches among them. I emailed him a few ideas, and he asked if we would consider moving to the city.

New York City? I had spent the last two and a half years arguing with seminary professors about how ministry needs were far greater outside America. Nichole had been preparing her entire Christian life for moving overseas. I had received clear instructions from God "to be the one Christian someone knows." Despite what many people think, New York City is home to many Christians.[1]

Even though we were far into the process to head to East Asia and had minimal interest in staying in North America, Nichole and I took a three-day trip to New York City to check it off our short list of options.

Searching for Malians

I had spent one day of my life in New York City—a Fourth of July excursion two years prior in which we fought crowds and witnessed a drunk driver fly off a New Jersey highway. Nichole had never been. But three months before I graduated from seminary, Nichole and I left our two-month-old son with family and stepped into the foreign land of the Big Apple. I had no idea where to find West Africans in the city, so I googled "Malians in New York." One neighborhood dominated the search string—Harlem.

We did not know it at the time, but the government had recently increased raids and deportations of visa-expired West Africans in the area. When Nichole and I walked through the African-American neighborhood of Harlem and conversed with mostly undocumented West Africans, our presence made some people nervous.

Seeing many African hair braiding shops, we stepped into one and asked, "Excuse me, are there any Malians here?"

Around eight West African women sat in the shop. Half of them ignored us and focused on meticulously braiding their clients' hair. Half of them looked at us, heard our question, and talked to one another in an African language before responding. One finally spoke.

"Across the street. Upstairs."

We crossed 125th Street, found a barely visible shop sign, and proceeded up a narrow stairway "portal" into West Africa where a dozen ladies braided hair and gossiped.

"Yes?" one woman asked us as the room grew quiet.

"Excuse me, are there any Malians here?"

Oddly, a tinge of fright and nervousness washed over the women's faces.

"Why? Tell me what has happened."

"Ummm, I don't think anything has happened. I am just looking for Malian people."

A brief stare ensued as the lady tried to discern my intentions. "Tell me what has happened?"

"Nothing. I lived in Mali. I speak Bambara. I've been to Bamako and Kayes and Mopti and Segou and Timbuktu."

She processed my response for a few seconds, then asked, *"I ka kɛnɛ wa?"* ("Are you well?").

I replied in the rhythm of a Bambara greeting. *"Tɔɔrɔ si te. I ka kɛnɛ wa?"* ("Absolutely no problems. Are you well?").

Immediately, a dozen African women whipped their heads toward us and responded in chorus, "*Tɔɔrɔ si te!*" ("Absolutely no problems!").

I turned to Nichole and exclaimed, "We found them!"

We exchanged greetings and conversed for a few minutes. Then I asked, "I see lots of women here. But where are the men? Are there any Malian men I can talk to?"

"Oh, they are working all over the city. But let me give you a number. There is a Malian man named Musa nearby. Tell him we sent you."

Musa

We called Musa, and he invited us to his workplace within the "B-Nice Discount Grocery" store. As we walked into the storefront, we noticed "grocery" primarily meant sodas, chips, cigarettes, and phone cards. We approached two African Muslim men who had stopped their conversation to look at us.

"Hello. Is Musa here?"

They pointed to an international money transfer business that had a small office in the corner. A West African man sat behind a thick wall of Plexiglas, a feature common in Harlem stores.

"Are you Musa?" I asked.

"Yes, yes, how are you doing?" he replied.

We greeted each other back and forth in Bambara. As is customary, perhaps to demonstrate one's belonging to a tribe as more important than a personal identity, he told me his last name first.

"That's a common name among the Wassoulou," I said.

"How do you know this?!" he replied. "I am Wassoulou!"

I was amazed. The Wassoulou are one of about seventy ethnic groups living in Mali, and they are one of the smaller ones. Musa was not only the first West African man we met in New York, but he was also Wassoulou! I explained that I had lived in Bandogo for a short time and loved the time I spent in Wassoulou land.

Musa had moved out from behind the Plexiglas and was grinning. "No!" he said shaking his head. "You speak Bambara and know the Wassoulou!"

He asked why I lived among his people. I do not remember how I answered, but my reply indicated I followed Jesus.

Musa gasped in astonishment, holding his hand over his mouth. Then, he said the unimaginable: "I am Wassoulou. And I'm a Christian who used to be Muslim."

Nichole and I were shocked. Not in Wassoulou land, nor in Bamako, had we ever met a Christian from a Muslim background who came to faith among the Wassoulou. "What?!" we exclaimed. "How? Why? How did this happen?!"

"Ohhh," Musa replied. "Come, let us drink some tea."

Musa locked up his Plexiglass office, and we walked two doors down to drink tea. Then, he began telling his story.

I grew up in Didiane, the biggest Wassoulou village in our region. My father loved me deeply, and he took me everywhere with him. We went to the mosque together where I learned to pray, and Islam entered my head. I started keeping the Ramadan fast when I was 12. The elders of my village told my father I should not go to school so I would be available to help him in the field, the custom for firstborn sons. Even though it made his farming more difficult, my father ignored the custom so I could receive an education and not end up with his difficult life.

I continued to advance in school, and because my region didn't have a full education system, my parents sent me to a small city outside of Wassoulou land for high school. It was there as a 20-year-old student that I became very ill. A doctor at the hospital said there were some diseases like mine that could not be healed. (I later heard that the doctor told people I would die within a week).

I went into a coma two times over the next couple of weeks. At some point during the second coma, I had a vivid dream.

I saw a large valley, and nothing was in the valley but bones, like the passage I later found in Ezekiel 37.[2] They were my bones. I was dead but conscious of what was taking place.

Then, a man's figure appeared among the bones, and he was shining with a bright light. He called me by name.

"Musa, do you want to be healed?"

"Of course I want to be healed," I replied. "But what about these bones? These are not signs of healing but death!"

"You will not die; you will live," he said. "If you follow me, you will live. Even if you face death on earth, you will live forever in Paradise."

"Follow you? Who are you?"

"I am Isa (Jesus)," he replied.

I was shocked. "Isa?! Don't you know I am Muslim?! They say we find salvation through following Mohammed. We are Muslims!"

Death scared me, not because of death itself, but because of hell. The Muslim teachers said that if young people died their destiny was hell because their deeds were not good enough.

Isa knew my fears, and he reassured me.

"Follow me," he said, "and you will not enter hell, but will enter Paradise."

I thought about his words and finally said, "I want to be healed. And I am seeking Paradise. If I need to believe in you to go to Paradise, then I accept."

At that moment, Isa disappeared, the bones left with him, and the dream ended.

When I woke from the coma, motionless and without strength, my mind raced with what I had seen and heard. How could I explain this to people?

My hope was in Isa, but I didn't know entirely what that meant. For us, Mohammed was the way, not Isa. But I made a promise to Isa to accept him, and I became stronger and stronger. One week after the dream, I rose from bed on my own. Within two weeks, I walked around town like normal. Within a month, no one would have guessed I had been sick.

When I fully recovered, I returned to the hospital to greet the doctor.

"Who are you?" he asked.

"I am the one you couldn't help."

"Eh, this is not possible!" he exclaimed. "There's no way you are alive. Who healed you?"

"Isa," I said.

When he asked me how, I explained that Isa appeared to me in a dream and promised to heal me when I believed in him. What Isa said had taken place.

"Isa?!" the doctor replied. "Musa, you have gone crazy. The sickness you had has affected your brain."

I defended myself, but the doctor had heard enough. He said I was crazy and dismissed me.

After that experience, I was afraid to tell people what happened. But when I traveled home, I told my father that Isa said to believe in him for healing and salvation. I explained that I gave a promise to Isa and that I wanted to become a Christian.

My father listened but then walked away to think. When he came back, he said, "Musa, I had no hope for you. I knew this sickness was too heavy for you. When I returned from seeing you, I told everyone in the village you were going to die. But now you are alive, and you say that Isa healed you. How am I to argue? If Isa, the one who has healed you, says he will bring you to Paradise, how can I argue?

"As for me, I am a Muslim, and I grew up Muslim. I have taught you my ways as a Muslim. But I don't know if I will go to hell or Paradise! If you are not allowed to enter Paradise because I insisted on you following my way, then I am to blame! If you say you want to change to become a Christian, then I will not prevent you from doing so. I accept this."

But my father insisted I tell my grandfather, who was a devout Muslim. He was not as friendly. He laughed, told me I was going crazy, and sent me to the powerful imam in our village. The imam was furious.

"This is Satan!" he said. "Satan caused your sickness and all this to take place because he wants you to leave Islam! But I will help you."

The imam wrote verses of the Qur'an with ink on a wooden tablet. When finished, he washed the Qur'anic ink into a cup of water, mixed the liquid, and muttered words in Arabic. He instructed me to rub the liquid on my head before I slept and promised that Satan would leave me. I walked home and did as he said.

But that night, Isa spoke to me in another dream.

"Musa, you said you would follow me when you were healed. Now you are healed."

"But Isa," I responded, "there are no Christians in my village. I don't know anything about Christianity! I don't know what I am supposed to do!"

"Leave this to me," Isa said. "I will take care of this for you."

And the dream ended. But this time, I kept it to myself and left Wassoulou land a few days later to finish high school in a different city than before.

Close to four months after my healing, Isa appeared to me for the third time in a dream.

"Musa," he said, "you complained about following me in a village with no Christians to show you the way. But I have now placed you in a city with Christians."

In my culture, when the same thing happens in three different dreams, it shows that whatever was shown in the dream is true!

The next day, I knew where to go. I had become friends with a Christian neighbor and schoolmate. That evening after school, I visited his home where he was reading in his bedroom. He greeted me and set aside his book on a table. I glanced at the page he was reading and locked my eyes on a line of text.

"Whoever believes in me will not die, but have eternal life."[3]

"Eh, what are you reading?" I asked. The words were like those Isa spoke to me. Of course, I had never seen a Bible. I didn't know my friend was reading the words of Isa from the third chapter of John!

My friend had never talked to me about religion, and he knew I was Muslim, so he hesitated. But when he admitted he was reading the Bible and that the words belonged to Isa, I was happy.

"Those words on the page," I asked. "What are those about?"

As my friend shared with me about the sin that all humans carry and the love of God that is powerful to wipe out our sin through the death and resurrection of Isa, I felt a peace, rest, and happiness I had never experienced. It was as if someone lifted me off of the earth into the sky. I was full of joy.

When my friend finished talking, I told him I was going to become a Christian and I believed everything he told me from the Bible. He was shocked and didn't believe me.

"Were you sent here to tease me or pick a fight? Or are you serious?" he asked.

When I explained I was serious, he continued in amazement. "I have never heard of a Muslim who wanted to become a Christian."

I told him about my sickness, dreams, and healing, even the dream that had occurred the night before.

"Eh, God is able," he said. But he still didn't believe me. "If you truly want to become a Christian, come to my home on Sunday at 8:00 a.m. to attend church with me."

Even though I constantly looked over my shoulder to see if anyone was watching, we attended church together that Sunday. I told the pastor my story after the service and that I wanted to follow Isa. I was baptized two weeks later. When the pastor gave me my own Bible, I read it cover-to-cover in a few weeks—both Old and New Testaments. It read like a novel. The Bible had all the answers for my questions. And you can imagine my response when I read the Valley of the Dry Bones passage in Ezekiel!

I experienced the weight of my decision shortly after my baptism. My host family kicked me out of their home, forcing me from one place to the next to sleep. I lived on mangoes and peanuts.

I returned home to Didiane during spring break and told my family I had become a Christian. All but my father were shocked and ashamed. My mom was angry and began to cry.

"You are crazy!" she said. "Why do you bring this shame upon us? None of our people have converted to Christianity! Life would have been better if you had been aborted!" And she cursed me.

The village elders quickly heard about my decision. Even though my father did not oppose my conversion, in our culture, he was forced to remain silent because my actions affected the entire village. The elders called me to their meeting place. They wanted to know if the rumor was true. When I confirmed my decision, they told me they had responsibility to bring correction to the village when needed. They ordered young people to give me lashings and a beating. The beating was so hard that an indentation can still be seen on the side of my head.

A friend of mine helped me escape the village that night by bicycle. We traveled around 35 miles to a city outside of Wassoulou land. Even though I had only two months left to graduate, I could not return to high school. So, I fled the country by bus.

In those days, communication was difficult between family members in different countries, so I thought moving in with my uncle in Burkina Faso was safe. But I arrived during Ramadan, and when they noticed I didn't perform the Muslim rituals, they questioned me and learned of my conversion. My uncle was furious.

"You came here for us to take care of you. But you are trash. That means you have made us trash cans."

He did not talk to me for days. I continued to stay in their home for a while, but my cousins cut up my Bible with scissors, and I was no longer allowed to eat out of the common bowl with the family.

"You are not worthy to stick your hand in the same bowl as us," they said.

Before long, my uncle kicked me out. But when he saw me at a neighbor's home a few days later, he came after me with his gun. I told my neighbor to run, but I stood and waited.

"My uncle, before you shoot me, let me say something to you." He lowered his gun and listened. "What you seek to do to me, I am not surprised. Jesus said that people who followed him would see their family members turn against them and try to kill them.⁴ But you also need to know this: Jesus forgives you. And I also forgive you. I am not afraid of death because Jesus has promised me Paradise."

My uncle stared at me a long time then replied, "I am not going to kill you. You are a kafir. I don't need to shoot you. Allah has already judged you." And he turned around and walked home.

I then fled to Cote d'Ivoire where I had family in multiple cities. By the time of my arrival, they had all heard of my conversion and said I had ruined our family's name. Not one of them welcomed me into their home. I had nowhere else to go. I was a new follower of Isa—and homeless.

I said to myself, "This is it. My choice is made. I give my life completely to God. There is nothing else for me."

Eventually, some Christians took me in, and I started a long journey that led me to study and work in the Congo, France, and back in Cote d'Ivoire.

I eventually returned to Mali, but I was never able to live among the Wassoulou again. Since fleeing the country after I was first beaten, the only night I have spent in my village was when my mother died. I lived in two different cities in Mali over the next few years. In both cities, I preached on television and the radio. Since I was from a Muslim-background but claimed Jesus was the way to salvation, I had many threats on my life.

Even though I did not reside in Wassoulou land, people from Didiane lived in both cities where I lived. The Didiane elders believed that if the young people heard that someone from their village had become a Christian, they would want to learn more about the Christian faith. My presence posed a threat, so the elders sent people to persecute me. I was the first believer in Jesus in the entire region surrounding my village, and my people felt shame. Whether from my village or from those threatened by my radio and television preaching, my persecution increased.

One day, I was riding my motorcycle. I saw two people rise from both sides of the road as I was speeding past. At the last second, they lifted a rope that struck me on my chest and flung me from the motorcycle. I was knocked unconscious. I spent a month recovering, but I lived. I still have pain from that incident.

On Easter that same year, as I was returning home at night from the church, I smelled gasoline and saw smoke coming from my house. I ran in to find all my possessions destroyed: my books, clothes, bed, everything. I was depressed and traumatized after that event. I thought, "What do they want from me? Is it a crime to switch religions?" It was difficult for me to return to normal activities. As a result, I left to live in Italy, but I returned to work in Bamako after 18 months.

I had no major incidents of persecution for a couple of years. But one evening, while coming into my home from the courtyard, I heard a gunshot. The bullet hit the doorpost right behind my head. I still have the bullet as a reminder. When that happened, I was so tired of the persecution, I wanted out.

So, I made the necessary arrangements, and two years ago I fled to America.

Mamadou, it's a miracle you walked into my life today. I became a believer 22 years ago. I have always felt called to be an evangelist to my people. But I have never known how, because it has just been me.

Nichole and I smiled at God and Musa. "Yes," we concurred. "This is incredible!"

I explained to Musa that, for the last few years, I had prayed every day for the first churches to be started among his people. I told him about my sickness in Mali and ensuing weakness, and how I had not seen a way to continue working with the Wassoulou.

"And now," I explained, "in a three-day trip to New York City to see if God was leading us here, out of over 1,600 ethnic groups in West Africa, the first West African man we meet is not only Wassoulou, but also a Christian from a Muslim background." I continued, "Musa, you are the only Christian from a Muslim background we have ever heard of who came to faith among the Wassoulou."

As if our meeting Musa was not enough, Musa then said, "You know, it only happens once every few months, but tonight, Wassoulou from all over the Northeast are gathering together in the Bronx. This is not a coincidence, Mamadou. Do you want to go?"

Several hours later, a Wassoulou cab driver picked up Nichole and me, dropped us off at the Wassoulou association meeting, and we all reminisced together about Mali. Some of these Wassoulou men had lived in America for 20 years without returning, but they met regularly for fellowship and to raise funds for development projects in Wassoulou villages.

After much conversation and tea, one Malian man left the meeting before business items were discussed.

"Where is he going?" I asked.

"Oh, he's not Wassoulou," they said. "He's not allowed to stay for this meeting."

"But neither are we!" I said, pointing to Nichole and myself.

"Oh no," they protested. "You are Wassoulou. You know Wassoulou land better than most of us in the room because we have stayed in America too long. We have forgotten! You are welcome in our association."

Decision Time

Nichole and I spent three days in New York City. We did not want to stay in America, but we could not ignore what God had done. He had directed us to the first Wassoulou Muslim-background Christian we had ever met. And despite being beaten and isolated, Musa wanted to reach his people!

The Wassoulou, however, were part of my story and not Nichole's and my story together. Furthermore, Nichole and I had both felt compelled to live in a place where people had little access to the message of the Bible. I had no idea where we would end up.

One week after returning from New York City, I picked up the mail and saw a package from the mission board to which we had applied. Our plane tickets had arrived for a conference to choose a missionary position in East Asia. Despite what we had experienced in New York City, we had not yet agreed on how to proceed.

Nichole burst through the front door that evening after work. "I have to talk to you!" She was smiling brightly, and the words leaped out of her before I could respond. "We're going to New York City!"

"Wait. Slow down. What?"

Nichole explained:

I was reading about the Ethiopian eunuch (Acts 8:26-39) during lunch hour today. In the story, the eunuch (from Africa) had access to the Bible. It was in his hands. He was reading. He had access! Despite that fact, he still needed someone to guide him. He needed someone to teach him in a way he could understand. It was only when he asked Philip for help that he came to know Jesus!

The West Africans in Harlem are the same way! Yes, they have access to the Bible if they want it. Yes, there are churches they could attend if interested. But who is guiding or teaching them? We have to go to New York and be for them what Philip was for the Ethiopian eunuch. We are going to New York City!

Nichole saw the smirk on my face and asked, "What?"

"Are you sure about this?" I asked.

"Yes!" she exclaimed. "Without a doubt. We are moving to New York."

"Are you sure?" I continued to smile.

"Yes! What? Why are you smiling like that?"

"Well, it's ironic," I said. "Of all the days for you to be convinced about moving to New York City, look what came in the mail today."

Nichole slowly took the package and pulled out our plane tickets—the same plane tickets we would have used to choose a position in East Asia, and the same plane tickets we would have used to fulfill the dreams Nichole had carried all her Christian life of serving as a missionary overseas.

"Are you kidding me?" she responded. She paused as she felt the weight of the tickets in her hands. "Well, it's good that God showed me we were moving to New York City before I saw these, because I don't think I could have made that choice otherwise."

Then, together, we ripped up the plane tickets.

---

[1] Researcher Tony Carnes estimates that up to 21% of New York City residents are evangelical Christian—largely because of Christian immigrants. Tony Carnes, "The Protestants of Metro NYC," *A Journey Through NYC Religions*, 5 Apr. 2015, www.nycreligion.info/protestants-metro-nyc-easter-day/, Accessed 21 Apr. 2017.

[2] Ezekiel 37:1-14: "The hand of the LORD was upon me, and he brought me out in the Spirit of the LORD and set me down in the middle of the valley; it was full of bones. And he led me around among them, and behold, there were very many on the surface of the valley, and behold, they were very dry. And he said to me, 'Son of man, can these bones live?' And I answered, 'O Lord GOD, you know'" (Ezekiel 37:1-3).

[3] John 3:16.

[4] "Brother will deliver brother over to death, and the father his child, and children will rise against parents and have them put to death, and you will be hated by all for my name's sake. But the one who endures to the end will be saved" (Matthew 10:21-22).

nyc

> For, "Yet a little while, and the coming one will come
> and will not delay; but my righteous one shall live
> by faith, and if he shrinks back, my soul has no
> pleasure in him." But we are not of those who shrink
> back and are destroyed, but of those who have faith
> and preserve their souls (Hebrews 10:37-39).

M OST MONTHS WHILE ATTENDING seminary in Texas, we were
forced to take money out of savings for expenses. The food
we ate during the week was whatever the grocery store had on sale
and whatever we received from a mystery food box from a food
distribution ministry. Sometimes the meats we received in those
boxes were mysteries unto themselves! When we received a notice
in the mail that our seminary housing rent was increasing 10%,
the increase seemed so high we started looking into other housing
options. But when we looked online at Harlem apartment prices,
the market rate for small, two-bedroom apartments was over four
times our rent in Texas!

Nichole and I don't remember worrying about the expense of
living in New York City. We simply trusted God in that if he called
us, he would take care of us. When an experienced New Yorker
asked about our budget for living in the city, he was appalled when
I quoted an amount that was half of what he believed necessary.
I countered that we lived simply, but we were obviously clueless. I
figured friends and family would provide some funds and I would
work part-time at Starbucks.[1]

Nevertheless, my vision of working as a barista never came to
fruition. Before moving to Harlem, a New York mission organization offered me a part-time job researching ethnic groups in the city.
Even though we were moving to the city to work with West Africans,

we did not have the means to do that work full-time. The Lord was obviously providing for us financially and, not so obviously, shaping our future in unexpected ways. I did not seek out a research job, but with my limited cross-cultural experience overseas, I was as qualified as anyone around, so they offered me the position. I accepted the offer but thought of the job as a means to help us do what we came for: work with Muslims. At least researching ethnic groups fit closer to what God called me to do than making venti triple skinny vanilla soy lattes (I had to look that up)!

West Africa Outreach

Nichole and I quickly started a weekly fellowship with Musa and a couple of his friends. To arrive at our Sunday evening gatherings, we walked 10 minutes from our home to the subway with our son strapped to our back, caught two trains to reach our Bronx stop, and walked 15 minutes to Musa's apartment. His apartment was located off a busy Bronx road on a dark, side street that featured an ominous canopy of shoes hanging from telephone wires. We hurried down that road, trying to avoid the scowls, glares, and comments.

An African friend later told me he lived in a ground-floor apartment on the same street. He said he slept for weeks under his bed because of the frequent gunfire outside his window. "No matter how cheap the rent," he said, "it wasn't worth it." Despite the rough street, the Lord protected our coming and going—and we often did not leave until midnight. Of course, some locals later told us, "The only white people ever seen on these streets are cops. So, don't worry about your safety; everyone thinks you're a cop." Since Musa's apartment was within walking distance of Yankee Stadium, some people stopped us on the main road and asked, "Are you guys lost? Yankee Stadium is the other way."

Our fellowship times were simple. We ate an African meal together, usually rice with peanut sauce or green potato-leaf sauce. We sang a mélange of songs in Bambara, French, and English. We read the Word of God in those three languages as well, discussing what we learned and how to apply Scripture to our lives. We talked about our week. We prayed together. In the midst of a city swirling with activity and the demands of survival thrust on immigrants, such fellowship times were sweet and rare moments to pause and remember why we existed. God had a purpose bigger and better than our plans or the pursuit of the American dream.

Our First Apartment

Our living conditions nearly killed our research work and budding relationships with West Africans. One seasoned missionary once told me, "Most people leave the mission field because of the gnats." He meant that small annoyances, living conditions, and culture shock take their toll, and those issues threaten the missionaries' longevity more than religious barriers, the people, or the task itself.

After deciding to move to the city, Nichole and I took another trip to secure an apartment. New York City real estate has its own rules and customs, and we discovered that finding an apartment was harder than anticipated. Most apartments required an annual income of 40 times the monthly rent rate. We were not going to make anywhere near that amount!

Nevertheless, we found an apartment in upper Harlem that looked promising. It was a 650-square-foot three-bedroom unit (small rooms!) that was lower than the market rate even for two-bedroom units. Even sweeter, it was a no-fee apartment, meaning we avoided the standard real estate broker fee of 15% of the annual rent. Much later, we learned that apartments list as no-fee when the owner is desperate and needs incentives to rent out less-than-desirable properties. We should have known. It's not as if we lacked warning signals.

When we first approached the apartment building, the real estate agent was fumbling through her keys when we noticed the front door was wide open with no one nearby. She apologized and said, "I thought they had taken care of that."

She scurried up the stairs, hoping we did not notice signs that a homeless person was camping out under the stairwell in the building. The walls looked as if they had 10 layers of paint—maybe more, as the building was over 100 years old. There was no elevator, which is typical of such buildings in the city, so we wound our way up the stairs to the fifth floor.

"Here it is," the broker panted while opening the door. We tried to ignore her expression because we wanted the apartment and its discount rate to work, but she was frustrated that the building's lack of security complicated her job.

The apartment was small but had recently received a simple renovation. Laundry would involve hauling clothes down five flights, down the street to the laundromat, and back up the stairs, but the price was right. And, the apartment owner was not concerned that we did not meet the income requirement as long as we provided a guarantor.

"We'll take it," we said.

The broker looked stunned but recovered quickly. "Uhh, okay. Let's fill out the paperwork."

A few days after we moved into the apartment, a loud hum awakened us as spotlights shone into our apartment. We looked out the window. An NYPD helicopter was scoping the apartments on both sides of the street looking for someone.

Several months later, we heard a racket outside. Our bedroom windows overlooked a large Harlem intersection. As soon as we looked outside, we saw a man waving a gun wildly in the air while people scrambled in every direction. Within seconds, several cops tackled the man from different directions. These instances were not just in our neighborhood, but on our block!

Within weeks of moving into our apartment, we realized issues in our building ran deeper than an insecure entrance door. A neighbor told us that a few days before we moved into the building, the superintendent's assistant was shot dead in the ground floor entryway.

We called for pizza delivery one day, and the phone call was routine until they asked for our building and apartment number. When they heard the address, their tone quickly changed. "We don't deliver to that building," they said. And they hung up.

Even though that phone call was odd, we did not think too much of the interaction until weeks later when we called a different restaurant for delivery. "Um, we don't deliver to your building," they said. "Our people get mugged there."

Sure enough, Nichole heard a commotion outside our door one day. She looked through the peephole and saw a Chinese delivery-man robbed at gunpoint. Our building was ideally suited for such activity. Besides the entryway being unlocked most of the time, the ground floor had a back door that rarely locked which led to an alleyway and separate street. People could enter one way and exit the other way without a problem.

A prostitute conducted business on our building's roof. She did not live in the building, but the building's maintenance supervisor gave her access. We talked with her on occasion, and she loved our son's blond hair. When we saw her on the streets, she enthusiastically introduced us to her friends.

A few months after moving in, thieves robbed several apartments in our building by climbing the building's fire escape to break in through the windows. While those robberies did not affect us, on another occasion, we experienced the invasiveness of such occurrences. When I was away from home, the prostitute's pimp attempted to break into our apartment with Nichole inside. She called the police, and the man left without breaking in, but the event was disturbing.

The homeless guy lived under the stairs for several months. He was friendly. We talked to him often, and he helped Nichole carry groceries up to our apartment without asking for money. Nichole made meals for him, and we had meaningful conversations. Even though he was a squatter in our building, he watched out for us. We had television-worthy characters and drama packed into a small building with 20 apartment units!

The drama, however, was not only taking place outside our apartment. Inside, mice were everywhere. No matter what we tried, we couldn't contain them. We plugged holes with steel wool and insulating foam, but the mice eventually chewed through them. They were New York City mutant mice! Our efforts to goad the building's management to activity were fruitless. They never answered calls or responded to messages. In our 11 months in the building, we killed 30 mice or so, but we were fighting a losing battle.

The mice, however, were the least troublesome critters in our apartment. I had heard the night time phrase, "Good night, sleep tight. Don't let the bedbugs bite," but I never realized that bedbugs are real—and evil. When we developed welts on our arms and legs that burned so bad we couldn't sleep, we investigated. A bedbug epidemic had hit New York City, and we were among the many infected.[2] Since bedbugs hide well and are practically invisible as infants, eradicating them is a nightmare. They are shadowy bugs that bite while their victims are sleeping, and the bite can't be felt for several hours! And, they only need to eat once every few months, so one can think they are eradicated only to be bitten a few months later.[3] We hired a professional to treat our apartment, but we still had to throw away items and wash all our clothes and linens. We spent a whole week carrying clothes up and down our five flights to the laundromat. To this day, bedbugs top the list of Nichole's fears.

Around nine months after moving into the apartment, a water leak developed directly above our bed. Apartment management never returned our calls. It was hard not to think daily about our exorbitant rent money being better spent on a mud hut in Africa! As I worked on the computer one evening, I propped my legs on the chair to avoid the mice that scurried underneath. I looked at the air mattress my family had been sleeping on for weeks in the living room because of the bedbugs and leak. My beautiful wife and son were peacefully sleeping as mice performed circus routines around them. We couldn't do it anymore. No matter how much money we lost on our lease or security deposit, we had to move. Soon after, we left and moved into a fourth-floor walk-up apartment on the main West African street in the city.

Survival by Grace

Looking back at that first year, I cannot explain how we lasted apart from the grace of God—especially Nichole. When we moved to New York City, we knew of no one doing similar work in Harlem or the Bronx. Our church fellowship consisted of a few male West African believers. Nichole is an extreme extrovert who draws energy from people. Most days, however, she stayed at home and dealt with the myriad of issues in our apartment. We lived in an unfamiliar culture, and I was away from home most workdays and some evenings to match the schedule of West Africans.

The winter was long and cold that year, and Nichole knew she was approaching a breaking point if something didn't change. She needed a social outlet with people going through similar sacrifices. Earlier in the year, she did an Internet search for ministries to church planters' wives. When she found one and inquired if they had a branch in New York City, the answer was, "No." But they encouraged and uplifted Nichole from afar. I was so wrapped up in my work and insensitive that I didn't notice, but without that group's support at that moment, I am not sure we would have lasted much longer in the city. God provided what we needed at the right time. Nichole's perseverance and sacrifice during that season astound me, and as I write, I am filled with gratitude to the Lord for my wife and his grace for helping us persevere through that year.

But our trials with Harlem apartments were just beginning.

---

[1] I do not know why I thought of Starbucks. I had never stepped foot in one, and I did not even drink coffee! I suppose it was the first business that came to mind as I imagined New Yorkers with nowhere else to go to meet with people.

[2] Two-thirds of hotels in New York City have had complaints from guests about bed bugs. "Reports of Bed Bugs in NYC's Hotels Up 44%, Survey Shows," *Pest Control Technology*, 12 Feb. 2016, www.pctonline.com/article/bed-bugs-hotel-reports-increase-new-york/, Accessed 14 Apr. 2017.

[3] In New York City, having bed bugs is the social equivalent of having leprosy. If known, people don't want you to visit their homes and people won't visit your home. One day, we invited people over who were excited about visiting. But when they heard about our battle with bed bugs, they wrote, "Something came up, and we can't make it. Sorry!" We never heard from them again. Some New Yorkers won't release infected people of their social stigma until a year or two of being bed bug free—and some never do!

little africa

13

*Now when they saw the boldness of Peter and John,
and perceived that they were uneducated, common
men, they were astonished. And they recognized
that they had been with Jesus (Acts 4:13).*

WHILE THE CIRCUMSTANCES OF leaving our first apartment were undesirable, the move landed us in the heart of America's "Little Africa"—Harlem's 116th Street. Decades earlier, this street had been the crack capital of the city.[1]

When men from a local church visited our home before sharing gospel resources with West African Muslims, one of them wiped tears from his eyes. He grew up in Harlem during the drug epidemic and had lived a reckless life, eventually becoming homeless. But in his hopeless state, he had found Jesus, cleaned up his life, and eventually became a leader in the church!

"I have been in your apartment building before," he said. "This was a crack house."

A man whose life had been transformed by Jesus found himself in the location of his past's hell, praying for heaven to come to the Muslims outside. Without us knowing, God flipped an apartment with a dark past to give it a new chapter as a beacon of light.

The apartment was in a perfect location for our work and, apart from a bad water leak that seemed fixed by management and the constant smell of marijuana from the floor below, posed none of the difficulties we faced with our first abode. The windows of our living room overlooked the intersection of 116th Street and Frederick Douglass Boulevard and faced east down 116th, the heart of Little Africa.

The block was full of characters and stories. One evening, I heard a commotion and looked out the window to see dozens of African men pointing at something in animated conversation. Nearly 100 people had gathered by the time I joined them, with the crowd spilling onto the street. Apparently, an adventurous raccoon had left Central Park, located a few blocks south, and was scrambling up a fire escape in fear. The West Africans playfully argued while trying to answer the following questions:

"What is this strange creature?"

"Where did it come from?"

"Can it hurt people?"

And my favorite: "Can I eat it?"

Those who favored eating the mysterious source of meat pretended to bring down the raccoon with slingshots, which are common in Africa for killing birds and small animals to "make the sauce tasty" for that evening's meal. If a raccoon had appeared in an African village, it would have been taken down in minutes. But this raccoon was lost in New York, one of the most efficient cities in the world. First, the cops came. Then animal control came. Then the Metropolitan Transportation Authority came. But none of them knew how to catch the critter, so they all left.

Seizing an opportunity for local glory, two African men took the matter into their own hands while being egged on by the crowd. Heavily armed with a sheet and a bucket, they precariously pursued the raccoon up a rusty fire escape. Each time the men neared the raccoon, however, the animal climbed higher, eventually reaching the third story. As the men worked the crowd to elicit cheers for a dramatic conclusion, the police showed up again and threatened to arrest them if they did not descend. We had been watching the ordeal unfold for two hours, but when the police ordered the men down, half of the spectators left, myself included. A couple of hours later, I heard cheering outside; apparently, someone had caught the raccoon. Not knowing how or by whom, however, we avoided dinner invitations for a while.

Little Africa

In Little Africa, Islamic sorcerers passed out business cards, advertising their power to cure sickness, financial problems, and impotence. Upon receiving a sorcerer's card one day, a Muslim friend spoke up when the supposed sorcerer was out of earshot. "Charlatan," he said. "He doesn't know sorcery. That's the problem these days. People come to New York City, and they need to make money, so they pretend to have powers. Most of these sorcerers aren't real."

Little Africa was home to dozens of West African-focused stores and community organizations. African restaurants selling rice and sauce, *halal*[2] butchers selling lamb, and grocery stores selling powdered milk and kola nuts competed for market share. Mosques did as well.

When West Africans first arrived in Harlem, they attended Malcolm X's old mosque at 116th and Lenox, a symbolic structure that mainly attracts African-American Muslims.[3] But West Africans had difficulty relating to the mosque's version of Islam. As a result, they started their own mosques throughout the city for their particular ethnic group or branch of Islam. From our apartment window, we could view the most influential West African mosque in the city. Many of the people who prayed at that mosque spoke Bambara or a related language. On Fridays, a slew of African cab drivers double-parked to attend the main prayer time of the week. Although several hundred people fit into the mosque, the crowds overflowed onto the sidewalks where prostrate men in neat rows declared their space in the city. Over 70 such West African mosques exist in the city to serve over 100,000 West African Muslims—most of whom are too busy to attend.[4]

While living in Little Africa, I spoke more Bambara on the streets than English. Everywhere I walked, I greeted African neighbors and friends from Mali, Cote d'Ivoire, Burkina Faso, Senegal, Guinea, Niger, and the Gambia. I knew where to buy the best *dibi* (grilled lamb), *mafe* (peanut stew), and ginger juice. I frequented Farafina (which means black-skinned) Coffee Shop to meet people and develop relationships.

I attended African association meetings, started English classes to help West Africans improve their ability to communicate and survive, and visited many homes. I told Malians and other West Africans, "Look, you guys are some of the most hospitable people I have ever met. You welcomed me when I came to your country (or region). Now, you come to New York City, and who welcomes you? No one! Hospitality is hard to find here. I want to try to do for you as you have done for me. I welcome you!" And we did, helping personally and also referring them to the many services available in the city.

When people leave everything behind in their home country—status, family, identity, and community solidarity—to move to a place like New York City the struggle is deep. The city can be a dehumanizing place in which people's background stories, skills, and identities are discarded for the rat race of commerce and survival. A welcoming hand restores the dignity that was instantly lost upon arrival. Simply asking people about their story, their home, and their former life—or even showing the faintest acknowledgment that such a world existed—are gestures powerful enough to elicit tears.

One day, a volunteer with our ministry wore an African dress from Guinea, a place she had never visited. Nevertheless, a homesick woman from Guinea passed by the volunteer, saw the dress, and wept at her feet. "How do you know this? How do you know this?" she cried.

I have to remind myself and other Americans that before visitors from Africa are Muslim or immigrants or illegal or however one views them, they are people. And Christ first and foremost sees them that way, as people created by God and for God who are to be loved and welcomed and cherished regardless of one's political or religious views.

Sadly, too many churches have become agents for spreading hatred of Muslims, which is odd considering Jesus's admonition to "love your enemies and pray for those who persecute you" (Matthew 5:44). One missionary associated with us recently planned a training seminar in a church on sharing Jesus with Muslims. The church leaders canceled the event a couple of days prior because they feared their members might begin associating with Muslims and, gasp, bringing them to church. Fear, instead of love, has infected too many churches' attitudes toward Muslims.

Muslim Friends

The greatest substance and meaning in life and ministry happen in the context of close relationships. Before long, some of my best friends in Harlem became a handful of West African Muslim men.

Ntogoma was one of the first Malian friends I made in the city. He sold cologne, perfume, and incense as a street vendor. We greeted each other a few times before we spent more time in conversation, first at his workplace, and later in each other's homes. A year and a half after arriving in the city, I took Ntogoma on a road trip from New York City to Texas and back, covering 13 states on one of his first views of America outside of the city.

At least once a week, Ntogoma and I sat together by his street-vending stand. As the craziness of Manhattan passed in front of us, we talked about the differences between our countries, living life as a foreigner, and our mutual distaste for *"to"* (a playdough-like staple of Malian cuisine pronounced like "toe").

As we shared life together, stories and lessons from the Bible flowed into our conversation. When Ntogoma showed interest in these stories, I asked him if he wanted to hear stories from the beginning of God's Word and on through the prophets. He agreed to do so.

West Africans, like many people in the world, are event oriented rather than time oriented. The relationship building aspect that preceded and followed the actual Bible study was desired, and even necessary, for any information from the Bible to be communicated and received. For many people in the world, the content of what is communicated is not as important as the character or status of the person communicating. How the communicator is viewed affects the weight or value of the message, regardless of the message's content. As a result, building my friendship with Ntogoma apart from the actual Bible study was essential, and I had to block off ample space for a "Bible study event" in my time-oriented calendar.

At the onset of our Bible studies, Ntogoma bought hot tea (his with two sugars, mine with none), and we talked about anything

and everything for an hour or two. Every time we talked, customers frequently interrupted Ntogoma to buy incense or knock-off
designer fragrances. Occasionally, radical members of a local, Afro-
centric religious sect passed by in matching robes, stared me down,
and called me "Satan." In response, Ntogoma shook his head and
consoled me. "Those guys are crazy. They say 'Africa, Africa,' but
they've never seen Africa. You know Africa better than they do!"

Eventually, however, our Bible story time began with Ntogoma
asking, "Okay, Mamadou, is it not time to tell the story?" And we
began, first reviewing the last story told and how we applied it to
our lives, then telling the new story followed by a discussion on its
meaning and application. The whole event usually took three hours.

One afternoon, as we finished our story time, a friend of Ntogoma's named Zoumana came to greet. When Zoumana heard from
Ntogoma that we were learning Bible stories together, he pulled me
aside and began talking in a hushed tone.

"I need to talk to you, but not here. Please come with me to
my apartment."

We gave blessings to Ntogoma as we left and weaved in and out
of sidewalk traffic to Zoumana's apartment.[5] Zoumana did not say
a word until we sat in his bedroom with the door shut.

"Now," he said, "I am excited that I met you today because I
want to learn about becoming a Christian."

"What?" I had just met this guy! "Okay, why is that?"

Zoumana replied:

*Well, I am from a small village in Mali. It is a poor village with great needs.
I have noticed for many years that Muslims have done nothing to help us, even
though our country is Muslim. But Christians came to our village, dug a well,
and helped in other ways. Christians have the true way. I have been thinking
about this for a long time.*

Thus began my relationship with Zoumana. Within the next few
weeks, Zoumana joined my Bible storying times with Ntogoma, and
soon a small group of Muslim men met with me twice a week for
prayer and Bible study. The way they viewed the world was slowly
changed by the Bible. They began praying in the name of Jesus and
living out the stories of the Bible in their daily lives. One evening,

I reminded this small group that they needed to share with others what they were learning from the Bible.

Zoumana countered, "But we do not know the Bible as well as you." I replied that they knew the Bible better than most Christians in America.

Zoumana pondered my statement then sat up with his back straight and exclaimed, "That's right! Peter and John were uneducated and ordinary like us, but they spoke with boldness before the religious leaders of the day about Jesus. We can do the same!"

Because our Muslim friends did not have Christian vocabulary apart from Scripture and were encouraged to pray in their language, their prayers were fresh and rich, filled with new ways of expressing themselves to God. Below is a condensed translation of one man's prayer, who prayed with emotion.

Creator God,

Help me!

Here, horrible!

Me, horrible!

I know how to count to 100 in English,

I know all the English words to conduct business,

But I don't know how to talk about you in English!

I don't know how to talk about your way!

What does that show about what's important to me?

Here, horrible!

Me, horrible!

I complain about money or a lack of possessions in my hands,

While you create the air that gives us life,

Did I pay you for that?

No!

You give it for free!

Here, horrible!

Me, horrible!

Put your words in me.

Put me on the straight path.

Here, horrible!

Here, horrible!

Me, horrible!

Help us!

It is because of Isa that we are here, and we pray in his name.

Amen.

Big Daddies

Zoumana's life in New York was the same as most West African immigrants. He worked as many hours as possible, lived as cheaply as he could, and sent most of his money to his wife and children in Africa. At one point, Zoumana worked as a car washer in the Bronx from 6:00 p.m. until 6:00 a.m., even in the winter cold. After returning home, he had only two to three hours sleep before his ten-to-five job at a clothing store. He repeated this schedule every day of the week but one, which he spent washing clothes and making up sleep.

I asked Zoumana why he stayed in New York. His answer was the same as most Africans in the city:

We come here because we have always heard of America. We think we will step off the plane and people will hand us money. Even if our people try to tell us America doesn't work that way, we don't believe them. We have to see for ourselves.

I had a rough season with finances, so I decided to make up for my loss in America. I planned to stay for two to three years and return. But once I arrived, I realized how expensive life was and how sending money back home was difficult. I met all these people from my country with the same plans, but had lived in New York for 10 years, 20 years. When we return, we have to return with honor. But if most of us returned now, we would do so with shame because we have not obtained what we desired. So, life in America is like prison. If we go back to Mali, everyone will come to us asking for money. And what do we do if we do not have any? So, we stay in shame, although we keep thinking next year will be the one when we return.

As we began to know and understand the African Muslim community in New York, we realized that they constantly talked on the phone with people in their home country. If they were not talking to people about financial problems, they were checking on the status of their homes being built, starting and managing business ventures, mediating family disputes, or simply staying connected. To maximize our impact in the West African community in New York, we concluded we needed to know their family and friends in their homeland.

So, two years after moving to New York, I returned to Mali for the first time after two previous medical evacuations. When Zoumana heard I was returning, he said he would take care of me when I arrived. In the back of my mind, I questioned what that meant coming from a car-washer in the Bronx. But I soon found out that Zoumana, who worked menial jobs in New York City, was a *mogoba* (a "big daddy") back home.

When Nichole and I arrived at the airport in Bamako, an influential politician picked us up at the airport. The politician was Zoumana's relative. The man escorted us to a middle-class neighborhood. As we snaked our way through potholed streets, we approached a large, two-story home enclosed by a tall, concrete wall.

As the gate opened into the inner courtyard, we noticed a Mercedes parked inside. Around a dozen men and women, including a woman wearing an elaborate African dress, came to greet us. The woman was Zoumana's wife. She owned the Mercedes and had returned that day from a business trip to Dubai. Zoumana's wife, children, and other relatives lived throughout the two-story complex. Distant relatives who cleaned and cooked for the family also lived in the compound. Zoumana had built and paid for his spacious home in Africa without loans.

The next day, Nichole and I traveled to Bamako's big market. Accompanied by one of Zoumana's relatives, we trekked through a maze of winding paths that squeezed between vendors of wax cloth, radios, bean fritters, Islamic literature, and knock-off shoe brands like Niky and Reebuks. We entered a store with beautiful

African cloth hanging from the ceiling and piled along the walls. Several men were busy making cloth designs, a group chatted over tea, and others displayed cloth to customers. This African cloth business was the largest of its kind in the big market and employed around 20 people. And we discovered that Zoumana owned the business.

One afternoon, as we sat in the store and waited for the manager, an important-looking man walked in and introduced himself. He was excited when he discovered we knew Zoumana. He explained that he was the president of an important business association in Mali and that Zoumana was the former vice-president! We also found out Zoumana owned two other properties that he rented out for income. He was my car-washer friend!

Upon returning to America, we had a whole new understanding of the lives of West Africans in New York. They had status and identity as big daddies (or big mommas!) back home, but they took on the suffering of menial jobs in New York City as sacrifices for their families.

My African friends lived in two different worlds: their homeland with their big daddy status, and America where they had little status. But what implications did that have for us? As we learned to relate to the African community, we knew we needed to make similar sacrifices with our status and identity. After all, we lived in America, but not an America with which we were familiar. Like my African friends, my family lived in two worlds at the same time.

---

[1] The Harlem crack epidemic is partly responsible for the creation of Little Africa. West Africans mass migrated to Harlem in the 1980s at a time when 116th Street was in shambles. With their work ethic and strong sense of community, West Africans found cheap rent along 116th Street and eventually rented a majority of the storefronts on a two-block stretch, effectively reviving the street. Naturally, they found apartments in the same area. Due to Harlem's recent gentrification, rents are increasing, and the West African presence in the area is dwindling.

[2] *Halal* denotes food permissible to eat under Islamic law or meat prepared in accordance with Islamic law.

[3] The Masjid Malcolm Shabazz (Shabazz was a name that Malcolm X adopted after his *hajj* to Mecca) owns the main West African craft market located down the street from the mosque.

[4] For more details and maps on the various populations of Muslims in Metro New York, see a nine blog series starting with Chris Clayman, "Muslims in Metro New York (Part 1), *Global Gates*, 22 Feb. 2016, globalgatesinfo.wordpress. com/2016/02/22/muslims-in-metro-new-york-part-1-one-million-muslims/, Accessed 14 Apr. 2017.

[5] At one point in the early 1990s, a five-block segment of 125th Street contained over 1,000 street vendors. The street resembled an African market, where one had to squeeze and elbow their way through. Hundreds of police cleared the street vendors in 1994 with the support of the 125th Street Business Improvement District. The clearing of the African-market-like 125th Street was the impetus for establishing the current Malcomb Shabazz Harlem Market, a West African craft market on 116th Street.

citizens *of the diaspora* PART I   14

To the weak I became weak, that I might win the weak. I have become all things to all people, that by all means I might save some. I do it all for the sake of the gospel, that I may share with them in its blessings (1 Corinthians 9:22-23).

WHEN MISSIONARIES LEAVE THEIR home to live in foreign countries, they give up cultural comforts and adapt their way of life to the new culture. They expect to try new things, eat weird food, and look foolish in ways they would have never done back home.[1] Because examples are few of people working cross-culturally in their own country, some missionaries and ministry supporters are surprised that similar adjustments are needed. In some ways, cross-cultural mission work is more difficult in the missionary's home country than overseas because the worker has not left cultural distractions and social demands.

Such difficulties are exacerbated with the knowledge and experience that work among immigrant unreached peoples rarely fits into the Body of Christ's pre-defined categories of mission. I have been asked on numerous occasions, "Do you ever think you will go back to the mission field?" Furthermore, churches often separate "foreign missions" among different people groups from starting churches in America (among their own people group) and don't know where we fit. Truth be told, we often don't fit into existing structures and categories! And we feel it.

When West Africans leave Africa for America, they are no longer fully part of the community in Africa, nor are they fully American. In seeking to share the gospel effectively with West Africans, even though we were from America living in America, we tried to live and act as if we had left the country. We attempted to enter a similar liminal state as our African immigrant friends.

With that mindset, we constructed values, schedules, and ministry plans that reflected our identity as citizens of the diaspora (the diaspora consists of the collection of people dispersed from their homeland). Those changes were evident in what we did: how and where we spent our time, where we lived, how we looked, how we related to the community, how we shared the Bible, and how we used our home.

Those changes also impacted what we did not do. We did not share important events in our lives only with those from our cultural background. We did not attend many of our family gatherings. We did not live in a community separate from West Africans. We did not assume West Africans would fit into American Christian structures, and we did not attend most mission conferences and churches to which we were invited. We found ways to adjust, even when other Americans did not understand, and that meant being the same fools we would have been overseas. We became "foreign" missionaries in our native setting.

Singing the Gospel

Being a citizen of the diaspora is difficult. It means I cannot control my schedule with exact meeting times, or pre-package my gospel conversations. I have to listen to people, understand them, and ride the rhythm of relationships and conversations. I experienced this dynamic early in our New York ministry when I visited two West African "praise singers."

In West Africa, there is a caste of people called *griots* or *jelis* who resemble the minstrels of medieval Europe. They are the musicians, historians, praise-singers, wisdom-givers, emcees, genealogists, and storytellers of African society. They are West Africa's collective memory, and they are present at almost every naming ceremony, wedding, and funeral. I have rarely heard *griots* speak. Instead, blessings, stories, proverbs, and history resound from their mouths as if they lived in a musical. Shortly after moving to New York, I frequently visited a *griot* couple. One evening as I sat on the couch with Kante (the husband) after a hearty meal of rice and peanut sauce, Sissoko (the wife) began singing to me while washing dishes.

"Ohhhh, Mamadou." The "oh" was stretched out, equally shout and song, to beckon my attention. Then, in customary *griot* fashion, she began to flatter me in song. "You are such a good person. Your name is one of the great names of Africa. You are powerful and strong. You are full of wisdom." And so forth. But she was trying to butter me up for the question that came next: "Why don't you become Muslim?"

I could have answered through normal speech, but Sissoko communicated truth through song. If song was her medium of communicating truth, and I had truth to communicate, why should I use a different form? So, I replied in song, attempting to mimic the vocal styling of the *griot*.

"Ohhhhh, Sissoko." I tried the part shout and part song "oh" to beckon her attention. "How can I become Muslim? I have found peace with God through Jesus the Messiah."[2]

When she replied in song, I realized we were starting a singing conversation.

I continued, explaining the gospel in the best singing *griot* impersonation I could muster. We sang back-and-forth for over 20 minutes. Out of all the times I have shared my life and the Bible with this couple, none was more powerful than that singing conversation.

We connected. We connected because I heard how they communicated, and I attempted to communicate in the same way. Even though the gospel message is hard to hear and often offensive to Muslims, Sissoko beamed as I sang that message. She heard me.

The Goatee

For most of our first decade in New York City, I have worn a goatee that extends a fist's length below my chin. I often hear that West Africans, on inquiring with one another if they know me, say, "You know, Mamadou," while acting like they are stroking a goatee. Some joke that I look like a billy goat.

Nevertheless, I have shaved my goatee off only twice in our first ten years in the city. The second time I shaved was on Nichole's and my 10-year wedding anniversary. I look so different clean-shaven that Nichole wondered what I had done with her husband, and when my kids saw me they cried. They wanted the goatee back.

The first time I shaved was a couple of years after moving to the city; it was a bad goatee day. I woke up with one end of the goatee heading east and the other west. Attempts to tame the hair through water or trimming failed. So, I tried to prune it like a bonsai tree, but eventually, the hair was almost gone, so I shaved it all. I did not think much about my shorn chin until Zoumana showed up for a Bible study with other Malians that evening.

As Zoumana ascended the stairs, he saw me about 10 feet out and froze as if he had seen a ghost. "What have you done?" he asked as if I had shaved off my ear instead of my hair.

"Oh, you know," I replied. "Bad goatee day. Hair was going everywhere. Tried to trim it but it didn't work, so I shaved it off. Don't worry, it'll grow back."

Zoumana pondered my explanation and inched toward the door, but he was obviously troubled.

Shortly after returning from the kitchen with the requisite tea and sugar, I attempted to begin our Bible study. But Zoumana, who was typically warm and jovial, sat like a new kid in kindergarten class while glancing at me out of the corner of his eye.

I stopped what I was saying and asked Zoumana, "Do we need to talk?"

"Absolutely," he said. "You should not have shaved your goatee."

"Uh, okay. I'm sorry. It will grow back."

"You should not have done this."

"Zoumana, what is the big deal about me shaving my goatee?"

"It's a very big deal. I think you traveled to Texas for Christmas," he said, "and you saw all these people who dressed nice, and looked nice, and had nice things. And you wanted to be like them. I think you stopped thinking about God, and you started thinking about what people think of you."

"Wow," I could have never seen that coming. "Well, Zoumana, I hear you, but I don't think that's the case. You know how Jesus told the Pharisees they were whitewashed tombs? Jesus was more concerned about the inside of a person than the outside."

"That is a good answer," Zoumana admitted, "but you should not have done this! Beforehand, Africans saw you, and they thought, 'Hmmm, he is a white guy, but it looks like he knows God.' And they became close to you. Now, they will look at you, but they will walk right by."

Zoumana's reaction fascinated me. Obviously, the way he viewed the world was much different from the way I did. I knew African Muslims attached religious significance to men having long goatees. A goatee around a fist's length often identifies that person as a religious teacher. I knew that Africans were more likely to accept me and listen to me talk about God's Word with my facial hair.

But Zoumana taught me a valuable lesson with his reaction. There is no message without the proper medium. Without having extra hair on my chin, Zoumana could not listen to a message from me. Even if I compellingly communicated God's Word in Bambara, Zoumana would have a problem hearing the message because of the way I looked. His worldview left me a choice. I could view his ideas as crazy and move on. Or, I could listen to him, and as long as they did not cause me to compromise godly character, I could adopt those ideas so the message of truth could be communicated, heard, and received.

I could have demanded that Zoumana overcome his discomfort because the message I had to share from God's Word was more important than my looks. We do something similar as Christians when we insist that non-believers enter our space to hear the gospel (our church, our Bible study, our evangelistic meeting, our way), which places the onus on the non-believer to overcome discomfort and fear to enter our world. But Christ, for a period of time, left behind his purely spiritual domain to enter into the physical and cultural domain of others, as uncomfortable and unnatural as that seemed.

If we have the opportunity to take away the onus of discomfort or fear from the non-believer and place those upon ourselves, why not do that for the sake of the gospel? So what if a restaurant waiter screams out a goat sound upon seeing me for the first time (which happened!). So what if I have to sing like an African *griot* to communicate! We can adjust our looks, change our setting, and work on our communication to make an important message easier to receive. Making these adjustments is part of God's Superplan. Paul said, "I have become all things to all people, that by all means I might save some" (1 Corinthians 9:23).[3] Sometimes, in embracing someone else's preferred medium, our love and respect provoke that person to hear a message they wouldn't otherwise hear.

First Naming Ceremony

Two and a half years after moving to the city, Nichole gave birth to our second child, a daughter. Americans, even American Christians, do not have significant rituals or traditions after a baby's birth. Maybe a photo of the baby is sent to friends and family announcing the news. If the family is part of a Christian tradition that baptizes infants, there might be a christening. Protestants who do not practice infant baptism often have a "baby dedication" at a church service, which consists of a pastor juggling a line of infants, praying over them, and giving the parents a pocket-sized pink or blue Bible to commemorate the five-minute event.

In West African Muslim culture, the baby-naming ceremony is one of society's most important events; it is usually held on the eighth day after a child is born. Friends and family flock to these events in their finest cloth of vibrant colors and bring gifts and blessings. The family of the child sacrifices a lamb or other animal, with a portion of the meat given to the poor and the rest for the festivity. Dates, sweet plantains, and ginger juice are also frequently provided. As part of the ceremony, the infant's hair is cut or shaved.[4] An imam usually attends and utters the *Shahada* in the baby's ear before announcing the child's name to the crowd (the *Shahada* is the Muslim declaration of faith that there is no god but Allah and Mohammed is the messenger of Allah). People with money hire someone to film the event and produce DVDs for distribution throughout the community. I have observed hair braiders in their salon watching hours of naming ceremony and wedding DVDs, commenting on who attended, what they wore, and so forth.

The West African Muslim baby-naming ceremony was unlike any ritual I had experienced in America. Nevertheless, I knew the birth of our daughter was an opportune time to share our lives and faith with our West African friends. To do so in a culturally familiar way, we decided to hold a baby-naming ceremony in our apartment.

We adopted the form of the Muslim ceremony and re-envisioned it for a Christ-following family. We happened to know a *halal* butcher who secretly read the Bible and loved Jesus. That person gave us a great deal on two whole lambs and six chickens and cut up the meat for us to cook. We had met a West African Christian from a Muslim background named Yusuf (whose story I will tell in following chapters) who led a group of African Christians. Some of those Christians came to our apartment early in the morning on the day of the ceremony to prepare food and drinks. They took all day to prepare the lamb, chicken, rice, and plantains, as well as ginger and *bissap*[5] juice.

When the event took place, we had lived in Harlem for over two years and knew many West Africans. We invited friends from our extensive list of contacts. We announced the ceremony in an English class we had started for West Africans. Yusuf informed his group of Christians about the event. That evening, despite the busyness of people in the city, over 50 people crammed into our fourth-floor apartment. There were people from Guinea, Burkina Faso, Senegal and, of course, Mali.

I started the ceremony by welcoming everyone. I thanked them for sharing in the joy of our new child. Yusuf, serving the role as Christian "imam" at the event, presented our daughter to the crowd and announced her name. Then, I told the story of the missionary she was named after, a person who faced opposition from religious leaders because of a desire to spread the message of Jesus to people who had not heard. I told how this missionary knew a cure for a fatal disease, of how Jesus's sacrifice cured the disease of sin that affects all humanity. Despite opposition, the missionary obeyed God and served others. We prayed our child would do the same.

Resembling a scene from *The Lion King*, Yusuf then took all six pounds of our daughter in his large hands, lifted her in the air, and prayed God's blessing upon her. Other African friends uttered their blessings as well. Afterward, we "chewed meat" (as my African friends say) and adults engaged in conversation as kids chased each other throughout the apartment. Several hours after the ceremony began, the last visitor left. By that time, the meat was chewed through, and lamb bones were scattered through our abode; Nichole even found half-chewed lamb in our daughter's crib!

After the ceremony, I was surprised to hear a small buzz was spreading through the African community about the event. I walked into one hair braiding shop, and a lady said, "Mamadou! I am sorry that I could not come, but I heard the ceremony was great. Did you produce DVDs of the event? That way all who were not able to come could watch!" I had not thought of filming the event, so I apologized that DVDs were unavailable, but I was shocked that people showed interest in watching such a small event.

Ntogoma and I were discussing the Malian view of morality several weeks after the ceremony when he said, "One way you know people are moral is if they are owners of people." By owners of people, he did not mean that people owned slaves; he meant that others flocked to those people and desired to be around them. Ntogoma explained, "It's like your daughter's naming ceremony. Many people wanted to come because they like being around you. The event showed you are a moral person. Otherwise, people would not have come."

Some people will question Ntogoma's understanding of morality, but his statement and those of others showed our experiment was worth the time and effort—even if our newborn's blanket smelled like lamb for a while. Also, the ceremony showed an example of how Christians could share their faith-filled lives with Muslims in a non-argumentative way, something Yusuf was particularly adept at, which is phenomenal, because Muslims had tried killing him for years.

---

[1] One time in Mali, Seba, my butcher friend, took me by the hand to a mud brick oven where he was roasting a goat. He had a big smile on his face as if he were treating me to something spectacular. Roasted goat would have been a special treat, but apparently I was more special than cooked meat. Seba pulled out the head, cut it open, pointed to the brain, and passed the salt. He ate one side. I ate the other.

[2] In the Qur'an, Jesus is called the Messiah (3:45, 5:175), but Muslims have no context for what Messiah means.

[3] "For though I am free from all, I have made myself a servant to all, that I might win more of them. To the Jews I became as a Jew, in order to win Jews. To those under the law I became as one under the law (though not being myself under the law) that I might win those under the law. To those outside the law I became as one outside the law (not being outside the law of God

but under the law of Christ) that I might win those outside the law. To the weak I became weak, that I might win the weak. I have become all things to all people, that by all means I might save some. I do it all for the sake of the gospel, that I may share with them in its blessings" (1 Corinthians 9:19-23). In another New Testament passage, even though Paul insisted that believers did not need to be circumcised, he had Timothy circumcised to better relate to the Jews (Acts 16:1-3).

4 The phrase used in Bambara for the naming ceremony can be translated as, "Baby hair cut!" The practice of cutting the baby's hair comes from Islamic tradition. Hadith no. 1519 from Jami At-Tirmidhi Vol. 3, Chapter 19, states that Mohammed's grandson Hasan had his head shaved with the hair's weight in silver paid to charity.

5 Bissap juice is a sugary drink made from dried hibiscus flowers. We call it "African Kool-Aid."

15

Yusuf PART I

If the world hates you, know that it has hated me before it hated you. If you were of the world, the world would love you as its own; but because you are not of the world, but I chose you out of the world, therefore the world hates you (John 15:18-19).

GETTING OUT OF THE way of the gospel as soon as possible is one of the secrets to successful cross-cultural missionary efforts. When no, or few, believers exist among a people group, Christians are needed from outside of the people group to proclaim the message of Jesus. This type of missions is the most difficult because the Christians are foreign, which makes acceptance of the message difficult. Once God brings a breakthrough and a trickling of believers begins, the outside Christian's role shifts to assisting local believers.

To arrive at that breakthrough point, the outsider Christian might spend decades learning to be an effective cross-cultural missionary, including years of training in Bible and missions, and years learning the language and culture of the unreached people group. All this experience is costly. But when the first believers come forth who genuinely love Jesus and share him with others, even if they have immature faith and lack Bible knowledge, they are infinitely more effective in the spread of the gospel among their people than the highly trained missionary.

The role of outsider Christians as evangelists is necessary in the beginning stages. When followers of Christ emerge in the community, however, outside workers need to shift their primary focus to training and equipping new believers in evangelism, knowledge of the Bible, and church planting. Of course, part of training people in evangelism is modeling evangelism. That process looks something like this.

Missionary: "You need to share Jesus with others."

New Believer: "I don't know how. I am not trained like you."

Missionary: "Come with me and let's do it together."

The missionary and new believer visit one of the new believer's friends or family members to share Jesus. The missionary attracts a crowd like a circus sideshow. He or she becomes the equivalent of a dancing monkey that gathers a crowd. "Come," the people say. "Let's go watch the crazy foreigner try to speak our language!" The missionary fumbles around with vocabulary and, despite extensive effort, training, and education, sounds strange and foreign when sharing the gospel.

The new believer finds a nice way to say the following:

Thank you, missionary friend, for showing me how to share the gospel. You are trained and educated, and I have the utmost respect for you, but you are unskilled at doing this in my language and culture. Yes, I am not as educated as you, and I have only been a believer for a few days, but my people are 100 times more likely to accept the gospel from me sharing the three Bible verses I know than through the babble exuding from your mouth. Please get out of the way, so my people do not see this message as foreign anymore. Let me speak, so my people can see that following Christ is feasible.

Okay, so not all new believers have that confidence. Many of them struggle with fear, insecurity, deference to others, and so forth. But the scenario above usually proves true. An indigenous new believer even with limited Bible knowledge, if bold and loving when sharing Jesus, is exponentially more effective at evangelism than the cross-cultural missionary. When missionaries understand this reality they willingly change their roles to help equip, empower, and embolden indigenous believers.[1]

God used a man named Yusuf to help me shift my role in ministry. Yusuf was not a new believer; he was also educated, once serving as an elementary school teacher in his home country of Burkina Faso, which is located east of Mali. Nevertheless, our relationship is similar to the one described above between the foreign and same-culture evangelists. I used to share the gospel weekly alongside Yusuf on the streets. Such efforts were usually fruitless as Yusuf deferred most of the sharing to me. During those same weeks without me present, however, Yusuf saw many Muslims grow in their understanding of Jesus and some commit to following him! I eventually stopped sharing the gospel alongside Yusuf. He did much better without me! But we started spending that weekly time together in focused training and prayer, which enhanced the work.

Today, Yusuf might be the most effective missionary among Muslims I know in America. His story, his faith, and his relationship with God inspire me to be more sold out for the Superplan of God.

Finding Yusuf

Yusuf moved to Harlem three years before we arrived in New York. Throughout those three years, Yusuf consistently prayerwalked[2] around Harlem, pleading with God to bring salvation to Muslims from West Africa.

Within months of moving to Harlem, I heard rumors of a Christian evangelist from Burkina Faso. I had no idea how to contact him, however, and being new to the city I did not know if the work of a Burkina Faso evangelist would spill over into my focused group from Mali. At the same time, Yusuf heard rumors of a white guy who was sharing the gospel with West African Muslims, but he had no idea how to contact me. A full year passed before we connected.

The year after our family moved to Harlem, a volunteer group from my home church in Georgetown, Texas, was helping another ministry in the city. They asked if they could assist me for a day. I usually do not throw a bunch of volunteers from places like Texas into evangelism with West African Muslims in Harlem if they only have hours to spare, but since they came from my home church, I felt obliged. So, I sent them to set up a table outside a Harlem store whose Muslim owner was friendly. The table was full of CDs and DVDs that shared the message of the Bible in West African languages, and the volunteers were instructed to give the resources to anyone interested.

When they returned that evening, they told me a man visited the table, thanked them for what they were doing, and explained that he was a former Muslim who followed Jesus. That man was

Yusuf. They exchanged information, and the volunteers told Yusuf I would contact him soon. I called him right away, and we met that night. We began a relationship that day which has not only enriched us personally, but has also been used by God as a beautiful partnership in the spread of his gospel. Yusuf is black-skinned, 6' 5" tall, and comes from a Muslim family in a country I have never visited. I am white-skinned, 5' 11" tall, and come from a Christian family in America. But we are brothers.

Yusuf's Story

Yusuf grew up in a small village in Burkina Faso, West Africa. Because his father had five wives,[3] Yusuf has difficulty determining how many children belong to his father. "I was around the twentieth child," he stated.

The people in Yusuf's village were known for their devotion to Islam, and Yusuf's family was one of the first in the region to adopt the monotheistic religion that spread into West Africa through Arab traders. Yusuf explained, "Mosques were everywhere in my village, but I never saw a church. I heard Christians were in my country, but I never met one growing up."

Yusuf's uncles had traveled to Islamic centers throughout West Africa for knowledge of the Qur'an.[4] What they learned, they brought back to the village, and Yusuf's large family established their own mosque and Qur'anic school in their courtyard. Before Yusuf was old enough to know about other forms of education, he gathered around his elders every evening to recite the Qur'an and write passages on wooden tablets. As early as four years old, Yusuf awoke each morning at 5:00 a.m. for ritual prayers in the mosque. Yusuf said:

> Sometimes, we were so tired. All the children prayed in the back row of the mosque. The elders couldn't see us, and when we bowed in prayer, some of us fell asleep without them knowing.

> For whatever reason, when I was six or seven, my father decided I needed a formal education in French. A new school had started in my village, so I was one of the first in my family to receive this type of education. Even though I spent daytime at school, we still spent the evenings learning the Qur'an.

At the age of 13, Yusuf was sent to a boarding school a full day's travel from his village. He was placed with a roommate named Jonathan, a Christian whose village was in the same region as Yusuf's. Yusuf said about Jonathan:

> *He was so special. He was gentle and loving. As a Muslim, I was taught to act a certain way to show I was strong, forceful, and a man. I tried to dominate and control Jonathan. I was so hard, but no matter how I acted toward him, he was kind. I was intrigued and humbled by his behavior. One day I asked him, "Why is your behavior like this? Why do you not respond to me with anger when I act bad toward you?"*

> *He told me God had taught him to be that way, so I asked him about his God. He then talked about Jesus Christ. It was the first time I clearly heard about Jesus and Christianity. By the end of that first year, Jonathan's behavior conquered me. I knew I wasn't behaving right, and I wanted to have what Jonathan had.*

Yusuf and Jonathan became close friends, even visiting each other's homes during the summer vacation after that first year. During the second year of school, still rooming together, Yusuf began cooking lunch on Sundays for Jonathan so he had food waiting for him when he returned from church. On one of those days in the fall, Yusuf asked Jonathan, "Can you teach me how to behave like you?"

Jonathan replied, "There is no way of teaching this. You have to have a relationship with Jesus."

Yusuf said, "I want that." Jonathan explained more about Jesus, about how he died on the cross for our sins and that our sins are forgiven by believing and following him. He described how Jesus was cursed but did not curse back, and how Jesus instructed us to pray for our enemies. "I could feel it," Yusuf said, "because I saw Jonathan imitating what Jesus did. He did not respond in anger when I was mean. I told Jonathan I wanted to become a follower of Jesus."

Shortly after, at the age of 14, Yusuf visited the pastor of a church with Jonathan and made a formal confession of his faith in Jesus. Yusuf began attending church with Jonathan, and the two friends often read the Bible together.

When school ended, Yusuf and Jonathan parted ways to return home. Yusuf said:

I was happy about returning to my village that summer because my life had changed so much because of Jesus. I wanted to inform my family of my decision. The first time I told my father about my faith, he dismissed me as if I was telling a children's story. But then he called me back to explain. He didn't show much response that second time. He called me back a third time to explain some more. I told him I attended church to pray, sing, and study the Bible. When he asked if I was sure about my decision, I explained that I loved following Jesus and that nothing could make me go back. I had found peace and happiness.

At the end of August that summer, Yusuf's father announced a family gathering. All the family members who lived outside of the village returned at that time. Yusuf's father presided over these meetings. Feasts were prepared, blessings were given, stories were told of their ancestors, and family business was discussed so as to ensure the family's legacy would carry on with honor. "My father was like a king," Yusuf explained. "Everyone brought him presents and money. Only later did I understand the great shame he felt because his own son turned from tradition to become a follower of Jesus."

After the family meeting had begun, with about 200 family members gathered around the courtyard, Yusuf's father called him forth. Yusuf explained:

I was shocked. I had no status in the family because I was only 15 years old. If I was called to stand in front of everyone, something was wrong. My father asked me to share with the family what happened to me during the school year. Everyone listened in silence. They thought, "What is so special about Yusuf that his father stands him up before the group?" But for me, I felt pleasure to share with my family about the peace, joy, and excitement I had with Jesus. So, I told them I had become a follower of Christ, and that I was full of love because of Jesus. I explained how I attended church and sang and prayed and read the Bible.

As soon as I said this, my oldest brother jumped up and asked, "What did you say?" When I repeated that I had become a follower of Jesus, he rushed toward me and slapped me to the ground. I did not know what was happening. I had never seen anything like this so I was confused. I stood up, and my brother repeated the question, "What did you say?" When I said again that I had become a follower of Jesus, he slapped me back to the ground.

My father, observing the activity, raised his voice. "Good!" he said. "This is the purpose of tonight's meeting. You know that as the family elder I carry the legacy of our ancestors. All of you are under my leadership. None of you are to change. If you do, you are against our family. Therefore, we come against Yusuf. Here is a young man with no status telling me to my face he has become a follower of Jesus. I can't believe it! I brought him before the family tonight to make an example of him if he did not renounce his decision."

Then, he asked me again about my decision. I don't know how I had the strength as a new believer to stand before my family and say this, but I told them I would remain a Christian.

My father shouted to the family, "Listen to me! From today forth, Yusuf has become a bad seed among us. To keep the bad seed from contaminating the rest of you, we have to extract the seed from our family. Sharia law requires this. I am not afraid to cast him out because I am losing nothing."

At this, my older brothers quoted the Qur'an and yelled that I was a kafir. They had violence in their eyes. At first, a few pushed me back and forth, but then, a mob of my own family began beating me, slapping me, and pushing me. They shoved me away from the courtyard, and I walked away. No one, not even my mother, came after me. They thought I would renounce my faith and return, but I could not turn away from Jesus, so I kept walking. I never saw my parents again.

Yusuf slept on the streets that night and walked 10 miles the next morning to a town where Jonathan's Christian uncle lived. The uncle took Yusuf in and called Jonathan's father. The rest of the summer, Yusuf lived with Jonathan in his village. Because the government paid for Yusuf's boarding school instead of his family, Yusuf was able to return to school in the fall. Jonathan's father paid for Yusuf's clothes and school supplies.

Yusuf finished out the school year and returned with Jonathan to his home in the summer. He returned to school in the fall, continuing to attend church with Jonathan. At the end of the school year, however, some of his family members showed up and asked the administration where Yusuf stayed during the summers. The administration answered the family members, and a delegation from Yusuf's family was sent to Jonathan's father. They threatened to burn his home down if he housed Yusuf again. In response, Jonathan's father arranged for Yusuf to live in the capital city, Ouagadougou (WAH-gah-DOO-goo), with one of his family members.

The following school year, Yusuf and Jonathan graduated from *lycée* (high school), and Yusuf returned to stay with Jonathan's extended family in Ouagadougou. But some of Yusuf's relatives also lived in the capital city, and they discovered Jonathan's family was still sheltering Yusuf. A delegation was sent to intimidate the family.

Out of fear of having their house burned down, the family released Yusuf to the streets.

At the age of 18, Yusuf was homeless. He slept on the streets outside a cinema in the center of the city. He took bucket baths at night by filling a paint bucket with water from a public well. Jonathan tried to help, but he had started attending university in another town. When he visited the city, he would find Yusuf outside the cinema and give him food and clothing.

Yusuf started working low-paying jobs guarding motorcycles at the cinema and washing dishes at restaurants, but the money was not enough to keep him off the streets. He enrolled in a university with a government scholarship and began attending classes, but the pressure, isolation, and homelessness weighed heavily on Yusuf. He dropped out of school, smoked incessantly, and shrank his life to one setting—a city cinema where he worked a menial job and slept outside its doors at night.

Jonathan assisted Yusuf every time he visited the city, but he studied abroad in Togo for five years, which made Yusuf feel even more isolated. Even when Jonathan returned during summer vacations and the friends attended church together, Yusuf did not feel accepted by the church. He carried the stigma of an outcast, someone whose family had left him and rejected him. Coming from Christian families, the people at church could not relate to, or even recognize, the pain of Yusuf's family loss.

Yusuf observed about his culture:

Community with the family is important. If you don't have that community or don't live connected to your community, it is better for you to die. You have to belong to a family to feel alive. I couldn't have that with my family. And I didn't have that community with a church, so the streets were the best place for me. I had nowhere to belong.

Yusuf had a firm belief in the Bible and Jesus and felt as if he could never return to Islam, especially after what his family had done to him, but his faith stagnated. He did not pray, he did not read the Bible, he did not attend church, and he often wandered the streets with nowhere to go.

Jonathan was patient and compassionate toward his friend. Even as a full-time student in Togo, he managed to send money month-by-month to Yusuf to rent a small room for shelter. The room was in a sparsely populated area far from the city center, but it gave Yusuf the option to leave the streets. Most nights, however, Yusuf slept outside the cinema as he had done for years.

Before long, even Yusuf's finite world of guarding motorcycles and sleeping outside the cinema was taken away. Three of his cousins discovered where he worked and came to the cinema yelling at him, "Bastard child! You are a disgrace to our family! Give up your foolishness of Christianity!" The three of them punched, slapped, and kicked Yusuf while hurling insults and watching him bleed. "We'll keep beating you until you come back to Islam or die!" Yusuf was forced to flee the area.

At 24 years of age, 10 years after his initial decision to follow Christ, Yusuf was ready to give up. He had been experiencing three months of excruciating pain in his stomach. He often spat up blood, and blood appeared in his stool. Yusuf described his state at that time:

> If you saw me, you would say I was losing my mind. I was becoming a crazy person. I wandered the streets. I stopped cleaning and taking care of myself. I was in so much pain. For three months, my will to live was slipping. I was asking for death, and I became comfortable with thoughts of killing myself. I thought the world was unfair and my life wasn't worth living.

But Yusuf was unaware of something. At a restaurant he frequently visited for rice and sauce, there was a young worker who knew Yusuf's parents. When the worker told Yusuf's parents he regularly served food to their excommunicated child, the parents convinced the worker to blot out the shame of their child and gave him poison and money to do so. The next time Yusuf visited the restaurant, the restaurant worker stirred the poison into Yusuf's water. Yusuf's downward spiral of stomach pain, spitting blood, dysentery, madness, suicidal thoughts, and faith crisis was unknowingly (to Yusuf) brought on by the murderous intentions of his parents. The only reason Yusuf came to know what happened was the confession of the restaurant worker many months later when the worker saw a healthy Yusuf on the street.

But before Yusuf was well, he was broken. Desperate and wandering the streets of Ouagadougou, a prayer awakened in Yusuf,

"Lord Jesus, I don't understand all this. I left my family, and you haven't done anything for me. If you don't do something, tomorrow I will go back to my family to be Muslim. I can't resist any longer."

That afternoon, in January, Yusuf returned to the room Jonathan had rented for him. He lay down on his cardboard bed as his life teetered toward destruction. He saw three paths before him: become a madman on the streets, return to his family and become a Muslim, or kill himself. But, somehow, even though Yusuf rarely prayed, he cried out to Jesus for help. Yusuf described what happened next:

> It was around 6:00 p.m., and I was awake. All of a sudden, it was like someone came and peeled off the roof. I could see the light and the fullness of the sky above. The light started shining into my room. At first, the light was distant and small, as if from a lantern, but then the light drew closer and more radiant. Finally, it was so large and bright it was like the sun itself had entered my room.

> I saw that the light was a man. I couldn't look at him directly because he was so bright. I asked the man repeatedly who he was, but he only responded by stretching out his hand. He lifted me up until I was sitting. With my mouth opened and still, in fear and at peace, I said, "Who are you?" But he let go of my hands and drifted to the sky with his arms extended. He went farther and farther toward the clouds as I repeated, "Who are you? Who are you?"

> Then, a massive index finger appeared and dipped into the cloud like it was ink. The finger wrote in a semi-circle as the light of the man ascended toward the writing. I kept repeating, "Who are you? Who are you?" And then the answer came in the writing of the clouds. In ink of pure, white cloud, the following words were written: Jesus Christ.

> I thought to myself, "I'm a dead person." That was my first impression.

> But then I heard the voice of Jesus from the sky. He said, "You think that you have chosen me, but I chose you." His voice was soft and brought me peace. I fell to my knees and said I was sorry. I saw he was behind all this, orchestrating everything.

> I vowed to Jesus that from that day forth, even if my family cut my head off, I would serve him and follow him. I would never go back to Islam.

On his own initiative, Yusuf found a church two days later and began attending. When Jonathan came to the city on a break from school and learned what had happened, he took Yusuf to the hospital. The doctors said Yusuf had been poisoned, but Yusuf did not hear how this happened until months later from the restaurant worker. Ironically, both of Yusuf's parents died within months of his vision, before Yusuf even knew that his parents had orchestrated his poisoning.

With Yusuf's improved health and resuscitated faith, Jonathan encouraged him to take exams to become an elementary school teacher. That summer, Yusuf passed the exams and received a teaching job in the suburbs. After eight years of living on the streets, Yusuf moved near his school, found a church, and began his new life in Christ—again. But persecution, dramatic life changes, and unexpected orchestrations from Jesus were far from over, as Yusuf would soon find out. (Yusuf's journey in God's Superplan continues in Chapter 18).

---

[1] Ephesians 4:11-12 are key verses for understanding the role of exercising our spiritual roles and gifts: "And he gave the apostles, the prophets, the evangelists, the shepherds and teachers, *to equip the saints for the work of ministry, for building up the body of Christ*" (italics mine).

[2] Prayerwalking is intercessory prayer in the same places people expect God to answer prayers. New insights about a locale and new spiritual contacts are often discovered because prayerwalkers are viewing their surroundings through spiritual eyes. See Steve Hawthorne and Graham Kendrick, *Prayerwalking: Praying On Site With Insight* (Nashville: Thomas Nelson, 1993).

[3] Even though the customs of Islam allow no more than four wives, in Yusuf's culture the youngest brother "takes care of" (marries) the wives of deceased older brothers. Since Yusuf's father was the youngest of many brothers, he gained wives through his brothers' deaths.

[4] Timbuktu in Mali, for instance, had an established Islamic university that rivaled Oxford and Cambridge and Oxford Universities in its antiquity.

*eth*N*Y*city

Behold, I am sending you out as sheep in the midst of wolves, so be wise as serpents and innocent as doves (Matthew 10:16).

MY RESEARCH JOB IN New York City was to create a database of the people groups in Metro New York, for the purpose of generating more intentional outreach to unreached people groups in the city. When I was first asked about taking the research job, I expressed interest as long as I was with people and not behind a computer all day. I was assured the job wouldn't take me away from people, so I accepted the position. A few weeks in, however, I realized my assignment would require me to spend most of my time in an office. My supervisor explained why the research was needed:

There are many denominations, mission organizations, and churches at work in Metro New York. They all follow the same basic strategy in starting churches: They work with whoever walks through their door. Churches start churches with a group of people who are already a part of their congregation, or among people who are of the same highly reached ethnic group.

Denominations and mission organizations do the same. A church planter walks through their door and seeks help starting a church. Maybe an Asian Indian pastor walks in the door of a Baptist mission organization. He says, "I was a Baptist in India. You are Baptist. Many of my people are here, and there are many Christians. Can you help me start a Baptist church among them?" The mission organization knows they should reach different nationalities, so they arrange funding or find meeting space, and the organization claims they are reaching Indians. The reality, however, is that the new Indian church might consist of an ethnic group that is not only nearly 100% Christian in their homeland, but also 90% Baptist! Just because a church from a different ethnic group or nationality exists does not necessarily mean the church effectively reaches lost, or particularly unreached, people.

When I look at denominations, mission boards, and churches in the city, I see us all responding to whoever walks through our door. I don't see us surveying and knowing the pockets of lostness in our city—especially pockets of unreached people groups—and evaluating our effectiveness based on how much we reduce that lostness. We don't even know who's here! Census information is limited. We need to know the major people groups that have migrated to metropolitan New York—especially the unreached people groups. Then, our evangelism and church planting can be intentional and strategic.

Once again, my naiveté came into play. My job was to document all the major people groups in Metro New York—where they lived, how they lived, and the status of their Christian witness. Looking back, I am convinced that no one who knew anything about New York would have agreed to such an overwhelming task. Fortunately, I was ignorant.

So, I started my work by finding what others had done. I discovered one scholar who wrote about New York City's immigrants, and I quickly read all her books and articles. A couple of months into my work, when I felt confident enough to explain what I was doing, I set up a meeting with that scholar. It was one of the worst meetings I have ever had.

"Come in," the scholar said as she beckoned me into her office. The office was on the 16th floor and had a clear glass wall overlooking midtown Manhattan. She glanced at me before returning to whatever was so pressing on her computer. "I'll give you 15 minutes," she said.

Even though I had introduced myself and what I was doing by email, I repeated my short pitch and requested any assistance she could provide.

"Well," she said, "frankly, I'm ambivalent about helping you. I don't want to help you because you are a Christian, and I don't like the purpose of your research. And, besides, what you're trying to do is impossible."

Her words stung. After all, who was I? This scholar knew as much as anyone about immigrants in New York, and she said my work was impossible. I tried to keep my voice from cracking and explained my research plan. Apparently, some semblance of knowledge, fortitude, and feasibility shone through, and the scholar's tone slightly changed.

"Well, it might be possible. Good luck."

And with that, our meeting finished before we reached the 15-minute mark.

Jesus once told his disciples, "I am sending you out as sheep in the midst of wolves, so be wise as serpents and innocent as doves" (Matthew 10:16). If we are following Jesus, no matter what our vocation or ministry, we will face wolves that oppose, persecute, and discourage. Sometimes they seek to devour us. We should not be surprised. Jesus told us this would take place. But we control how we respond. As life sucking as that meeting could have been, God used it to motivate me throughout my research and to depend on him more. My task was impossible. That did not mean give up; that meant God needed to work miracles as I plodded ahead—a common scenario in God's Superplan.

The first miracle happened that same day. I had come across the work of another scholar named Tony. He wrote extensively on religion and immigrant groups in New York City. Tony responded quickly to my request for a meeting and, by chance, chose a meeting time on the same day of my visit with the "ambivalent" scholar.

I had no idea what to expect, especially after my experience that morning, and I knew nothing of Tony's background. I arrived on the steps of the New York Public Library to meet him. As I walked past a giant lion statue and surveyed the crowd, a man with a stack of books and papers made eye contact. He called out, "Are you Chris?"

He was warm and talkative, obviously intelligent but the type with people skills as well. By the time our meeting finished, I had discovered Tony was not only an accomplished scholar on immigrants and religion, but also an elder in one of the largest evangelical churches in the city. And, he was working on a religious census of New York City, documenting every religious site in the city street-by-street.

"I think we can help each other," he said. "Do you want to come with me once or twice a week as I travel through major immigrant areas and interview religious leaders?"

On the same day, I had one of the worst and one of the best meetings of my life. Over the next few years, Tony became an invaluable mentor and friend. On the same day a scholar told me my research was impossible, God sent another scholar to guide me, teach me, show me, and make my work possible.

Before long, my research became more than a means to pay for our work among West Africans. It became an equal calling. As I created a database of people groups, I started realizing the significance and opportunity of reaching the nations through the city. Some ethnic groups—such as the Bukharan Jews from Uzbekistan[1]—had a larger population in one neighborhood of Queens than in the country from which they came!

As I documented ethnic groups in the city with little or no Christian presence, I was shocked that most of them had little or no relationship with followers of Jesus. Followers of Christ were missing an opportunity to befriend and love peoples who came from some of the most challenging regions in the world for Christians to access. Even though those unreached peoples made the task of going to the nations much easier for American Christians, having come to our country at their own expense while striving to learn our language and culture, we still ignored Christ's mandate to reach them with the gospel. But most Christians in New York and the rest of America were not even aware such an opportunity existed. I had been one of them!

God Provides Help

I had no budget for my research. I was paid for three days of research a week, but beyond that, no money was available. So, I purchased dozens of books myself, read over 10 years of archived New York Times articles on immigrants in the city, and found whatever I could on the Internet and from local and national government entities. I spent one to two days a week on the streets doing interviews and making observations in immigrant-concentrated neighborhoods. I shared tea with Muslim missionaries from Somalia wanting to establish Sharia law in America, observed food offerings and prayers in Hindu temples, toured a Taliban-supporting Afghan mosque, and had conversations with Vodou priestesses, Buddhist monks, Rastafarians, Sikhs, Jains, Jews, and a Korean Christian who dreamed of building a skyscraper with each floor hosting churches in different languages.

Yet no matter how much effort I made, there was no way on my own to do enough surveys in a couple of years to obtain an accurate snapshot of the status of Christian witness among all major ethnic groups in Metro New York. Like Abraham following the Lord out of Ur to the obscure land God would show him (Genesis 12:1), I was on a spiritual journey with God through my research, not knowing where I would end up or how I would arrive there.

Step by step, God plotted the way forward in his Superplan. My second summer in New York City, a professor from a large Christian school brought college students to New York City for a two-week intensive social research class. He heard about my ethnic group surveys and restructured his class to help me with my project. College students were less intimidating to immigrant religious leaders than a Christian denominational employee like me, so they were invaluable in gaining access to community leaders. The professor has brought students to the city to help me almost every summer since.

Churches and universities sent me college students to help me for weeks at a time, and even for whole semesters. People across America volunteered to assist with background Internet research. All the while, I added database information on all the people groups we discovered in the city. When I obtained a good grasp of the major ethnic and nationality groups present, I stopped adding groups, but not before my list numbered almost 500 distinct ethnic communities.

In a conversation with Tony one day, he urged me to write a book on what I was finding. I had already begun creating and distributing digital people group profiles, but I knew if I wanted the research to influence others, I needed to heed Tony's advice. I also knew that producing a book was complicated. I needed quality photographs of each people group, an engaging book design, and a large number of written people group profiles. And, I still had no budget!

I contacted an organization that funds college missionary interns to make an odd request for photographers. Such a request
was new for them, but they published the request and sent me two
experienced photographers. Those photographers took thousands
of photographs among dozens of people groups in the few months
they spent in the city. I compiled an exhaustive list of ethnic parades
and festivals in New York City to aid my photographers, and they
attended most of them.

Once the photographs and writing started coming together,
I still had the problem of designing a book with no budget. In
an initial interview with one of my summer research interns, I
discovered she was an aspiring graphic designer. She also needed
to complete a project to graduate, and designing a book exceeded
her project's requirements.

So, without any funds, our book was designed with the help of
professional guidance from the intern's professors. Another mission
organization heard of our project and volunteered their graphic design team to create our book cover. Overall, more than 100 people
volunteered time to help me research, write, photograph, or design.
Some people volunteered days of work, others months. God gave
me a larger staff of assistants than I could have compiled with a
budget. Sometimes in God's Superplan, our lack of resources drives
us to depend on God more, and when we need him more, we often
witness his miracles of provision.

Overcoming Final Obstacles

Over a period of three years, I had produced thousands of pages
of notes. I had created hundreds of people-group files on my computer with research notes, GIS maps (shaded maps of the city that
indicated where people groups lived), photographs, and more. I
had completed dozens of people-group profiles and had narrowed
the focus of my book down to 82 profiles. The research part of my
project was complete enough to finish a book. All I needed to do
was finish writing.

But about that time, the supervisor who hired me for the research
project was let go from his job. He was supposed to be the one to
put into action all we had learned. My post-research plan was to
focus full time on West African ministry. I felt as if I had built an

ark at Noah's instruction, only to find Noah had left. My supervisor's departure made me wonder if my three years of work was worthless. Our research was only worthwhile if people acted on it to prioritize ministry resources for work among unreached peoples. My supervisor was the only one I knew who was ready for such a task, and he was suddenly gone.

But the situation was worse than my supervisor's departure. The mission organization that funded my efforts called me to talk. They explained they had grown impatient with the research but loved my work with West Africans. They made the decision to cut off research funds but wanted to divert those funds to help me work full time with West Africans. I explained I was at the fruitful stage of writing about the research, but they said the decision was final. It made no sense to me. I was about to produce a significant and groundbreaking resource, but the organization that commissioned my work seemed to discard it before I could share the results.

I knew what I needed to do, but I did not like it. The research was hard enough while working simultaneously with West Africans and maintaining a family life, but the only way to complete the book was to work on it as an extracurricular activity. The book needed to be completed. The discoveries were too important. I told my mission organization of my intention. "You can do whatever you want on your own time," they said. I finished the project a year later. I often worked 20 hours a week on the book project beyond my full-time work with West Africans. I kept telling Nichole the light was at the end of the tunnel, but the tunnel felt long and dark, and the trials kept coming.

I had one-quarter of the book written, and I knew I could not drag the project on for years. But what could I do? Not only was I without a budget, but I was also crunched for time. One day, I taught a missions class in Manhattan as part of the *Perspectives on the World Christian Movement* course.[2] At some point, I gave a brief description of my work, including the book project. At the end of the class, a woman named Meredith Lee introduced herself and said, "I have professional research experience; I've lived all my life in Metro New York; I have experience working with refugee resettlement in the area; I'm a writer, and I don't have a job right now. Can I volunteer time to help you?"

I am not sure if or when the book would have been completed without God sending Meredith. I gave Meredith some guidelines, notes, and what I had in mind, and had her draft one of the people-group profiles. Her work was superb, and I saw an opportunity to reach the end of the tunnel. I returned to my mission organization. My new supervisor had shown more interest in my research and had become an advocate. For the first time, I asked for money for my book project. I asked if they could pay Meredith to help me complete the ethnic profiles. The same organization that had seemingly dismissed my research now came back and helped fund Meredith. With her help on 36 of the 82 people group profiles in the book, a prompt completion of the book became feasible.

I had tentatively called my book "EthniCity," but somewhere in email correspondence with potential publishers, one of them called the book "EthNYcity." I liked that title better and settled on *ethNYcity: The Nations, Tongues, and Faiths of Metropolitan New York*.[3] The latter part of the title is a nod to Revelation 7:9-10 which describes multitudes in heaven praising God from every nation, tribe, people, and language.

Since my book was aimed at a niche market (Christians who wanted to learn about, pray for, or minister among people groups in Metro New York), publishing options were limited. Furthermore, I had begun looking for a publisher shortly after an economic crisis in America. Literary agents and publishers told me, "These days, publishers won't consider a new author unless he is the pastor of a megachurch or can otherwise guarantee large sales." I inquired with every publisher I could find that might be interested, but none were willing to pay for color printing, a feature that was necessary due to the book's people-group photographs.

After four years of work, when all my options for printing were exhausted, God provided a way. These provisions seem ordinary in God's Superplan! In a random meeting with a ministry leader in New York, he told me of a group of Christians who were visiting the city a few days later that might be interested in my project. After experiencing months of failed attempts at finding a publisher, that group decided to print my book within hours of my proposal.

Shortly after, *ethNYcity* was published, and sales far exceeded anyone's expectations. All proceeds have been invested in evangelism and church planting in Metro New York. The book has inspired others in cities throughout North America and around the world to research their own city's people groups, and some have produced similar resources.[4] The book gave a "face to lostness" in the city and described which Christian populations in the city are best equipped to relate to specific unreached peoples. We realized our research created awareness of unreached peoples, and awareness created a sense of responsibility in local churches.

I learned of a Ghanaian church convicted of their church's ethnocentricity and how they prayed through a different *ethNYcity* profile every Sunday morning. I received an email from an Indian pastor claiming his Indian church members talked about Bobover Jews for an hour and prayed over their church's prejudice, sin, and lack of evangelism, asking God to give them his love for the Jewish people. I heard how Christians started spiritual conversations with people from different ethnic groups because of the knowledge and passion they gained from the book.

Knowing the stories of Metro New York's peoples gave me a deep love for the city. People often talk about loving New York City, but they usually reference New York's energy, job opportunities, institutions, food, entertainment, and other inanimate objects. But to truly love New York City, one must love its people. Those people come from hundreds of people groups, each with fascinating stories of why they, or their ancestors, left the only world they had known for a city that was more of an idea than a place.

The stories of Metro New York's people groups helped me gain a deeper love for the city's people, and what I learned from the research shaped our ministry's trajectory in ways I could not have imagined. But something in me still loved stepping out of the fast pace of New York City, and two flights and two days later, sipping tea in a Malian village where time stood still. The Lord was working in those mud hut villages, and some of those ministry doors could only be opened from Manhattan.

---

[1] Chris Clayman and Meredith Lee, "Bukharan Jews," *ethNYcity: the Nations, Tongues, and Faiths of Metropolitan New York* (New York City: Metropolitan New York Baptist Association, 2010) 178.

[2] These Perspectives classes are as influential as anything I know for helping shape Christians to live for God's plan instead of their own. They are held all over the world. For more information, visit www.perspectives.org.

[3] Available at: www.globalgates.info/resources.

[4] See for example, Hannaman, Gutierrez, Overstreet, and Ho, eds., *EthnoLA: Reaching the Nations, Tongues, and People of the Greater Los Angeles Metro Area* (Temecula, CA: Global Recordings, 2017). Available at www.EthnoLA. com.

 17

The heart of man plans his way, but the Lord
establishes his steps (Proverbs 16:9).

TWO YEARS AFTER MOVING to New York, I returned to Mali. The two previous trips to Mali with two corresponding medical evacuations weighed heavily on my mind. As became my custom before trips to Africa, I reviewed my current projects and computer password with my supervisor, and I reviewed bank account and insurance information with my wife. These were not dramatic moments with tears in our eyes. The moments were more like informing a friend or loved one of a new mole spotted on one's neck, not worth mentioning except for the faint possibility of a negative outcome.

I did not know how my body would respond to Mali. Even though my strength had returned, I still had digestive issues. As a result, I took precautionary measures. I visited during the cool season when there were fewer mosquitoes. I only drank bottled water. I took a more effective malaria prophylaxis. And I came loaded with mosquito spray containing DEET.

I have visited Mali five times since moving to New York, and with the occasional help of antibiotics, have left all five times without a medical evacuation. I stayed with families of Malian friends from New York while in Bamako, and I stayed in my old village of Bandogo and Musa's village Didiane while in Wassoulou land. Even though I still had missionary friends in Mali, on some trips I never saw them due to a full schedule of visiting the families of New York friends from Africa.

Like Zoumana, most Malians in New York are big daddies or big mommas. And I was interested to see if these influencers opened doors for the gospel in their home country. I had already witnessed their eagerness to send CDs and DVDs of Bible stories in their languages back to their families. The big daddies and big mommas are gatekeepers for their families, and since they are exposed to new ideas, products, beliefs, education, and worldviews abroad, they function as filters for what influences their families. Of course, some influences are beyond their control,[1] but they send products and ideas back home that have their approval.

One Muslim storeowner in Harlem, after receiving an evangelistic DVD called *More than Dreams* in French,[2] immediately played the DVD on the store's flat-screen monitor. He became silent, his eyes widened, and his mouth dropped. "I have to send this to my country," he said. "Wow. I can't do anything but watch. Our people need to see this." He made similar statements about the *JESUS* film. As a Muslim, he not only passed out these resources to other Muslims in his store, but he also sent a few to his family in Cote d'Ivoire. I had to keep my Muslim "dealers" of God's Word regularly stocked!

When I stayed with a family in Bamako, I noticed these urban women had more leisure time than women in villages. They owned time-saving household appliances and provided living space to family members from villages in exchange for household help. Missionaries in West Africa constantly talked about the difficulty of starting Bible studies with Muslim women because of their workloads. "Come and visit the wives of my New York friends," I told one missionary. "They are like men sometimes. They just sit around and drink tea!" Sure enough, one missionary came to visit, and even though she had struggled for years to start a Bible study with Muslim women in the city, she began one with the wives of my friends within a week. New York relationships proved to open doors in Africa.

Didiane (Musa's Village)

I didn't know what to expect when Nichole and I first visited Musa's village (Didiane) along with Paul, a Malian Christian from a Muslim background. We had finished visiting Bandogo and rejoiced at God's work in that village. A missionary friend had begun working with the Wassoulou remotely and eventually started a mission organization called Mission 10:14 to support the work.[3] Around 15 Wassoulou had come to Christ in the previous months and a church had formed, the first one among the Wassoulou! The village chief in Bandogo was reading or listening to the Bible daily and even had a dream in which Jesus promised salvation if the chief followed him.

But the seed of God's Word had been sown for years in Bandogo. Didiane, on the other hand, had almost no exposure to Christians and had driven their own son Musa from the village. Musa had heard, however, that his main persecutors had died and that people in his village wanted to know about Jesus. Paul, Nichole, and I were eager to see how God was at work.

We slowly entered the village in a four-wheel-drive pickup truck. Dozens of children ran alongside us slapping the truck and shouting in excitement until we parked. They encircled us, clamoring to touch our skin and begging for pens or candy. A group of elders sat nearby on an elevated platform of logs. Many had rotten teeth from years of kola nut chewing, tea drinking, and lack of dental care. We exchanged greetings and blessings with the elders and sat down. After a few minutes of small talk, a spokesman for the village raised his voice.

"My brothers!" he said.

"We hear you," we replied.

"Your arrival pleases us. What is the reason for your visit?"

"I am Musa's friend from New York City," I explained. "I send his greetings to you and have come to visit you and his family. He wishes peace and health upon you and misses you."

The elders asked about Musa's health, and from their smiling reactions, one would never have guessed that a similar group had beaten Musa mercilessly over 20 years earlier. They sent someone to find Musa's half-brother Ahmed, and we walked together to greet the village chief. Over tea, the village chief explained that Musa was one of two village sons who had moved to New York. He urged us to tell Musa not to forget his village. Many elders expressed their desire for Musa to return, but this time because of potential financial gain instead of feeling the need to "correct" him with a beating.[4] After our visit, we were ushered to the village guesthouse to unload our luggage. After a short while, Ahmed appeared and took us to his courtyard.

Musa had occasionally sent money to his village. He had built a small house in his family's courtyard where Ahmed lived, and Musa had even sent money to stock Didiane's pharmacy at times. Musa's presence in New York appeared to have given him an honorable status in the village, replacing the shameful one he had received upon conversion that provoked village elders to violence. We greeted Ahmed's family and ate a simple dinner from the common bowl. I had recorded a greeting from Musa to his half-brother and played the message for Ahmed on a portable DVD player. Musa encouraged him to listen to the words of Jesus and to seek out the truth in the Bible. After watching the greeting, Ahmed said, "I have wanted to know more about the Bible, but no one is here to teach me."

On that first trip back to Mali, we only had time to visit Didiane for one night. We anticipated our arrival might prompt a large gathering of people into the center of the village with djembe music and pageantry, but without alerting the village of our visit, they were not prepared for such an event. We felt compelled to share the gospel with the people of Didiane, but as the evening wore on, we realized such an opportunity would not take place in a formal gathering. Paul, Nichole, and I prayerwalked the village asking God to give us an opportunity.

After a while, a man greeted us at the entrance to his courtyard and invited us in for tea. The courtyard was the largest we had seen in the village. After we had greeted, we discovered the man was Musa's cousin. We talked for a few more minutes and told him we had a video greeting from Musa to the village. Instead of watching the greeting immediately, he insisted we wait until he gathered a crowd.

He took us to the other end of the courtyard. "This is the village movie theater," he said. "I play DVDs here powered by a car battery." Behind the open area with the TV were 10 rows of crude benches. They looked like church pews I had seen in rural villages. "Wait here," the cousin said. "We will tell people to come. Many people don't know you are here."

Men, women, and children trickled into the theater seating. When a crowd of around 50 gathered, I began to address them. "I send you greetings from New York City," I said. People laughed when they heard what resembled Bambara out of my mouth. "And I send you greetings from Musa. He's my good friend."

The young people showed no reaction to Musa's name, but the older ones leaned forward, straining to make sure they understood as much as possible of my strangely accented Bambara. Musa, despite the persecution from village elders, was well liked by his peers. His childhood best friend had even been elected mayor of the district.

"I have brought a video of Musa greeting you. He wishes he was here in person, but he was excited he could greet you in this way."

People kept piling onto the benches. As was the custom, the women and children gave up their seats to the men and sat down to the side. I showed Musa's 10-minute greeting and the crowd hung on every word. Beyond the typical greetings and blessings, Musa explained the impact of Jesus on his life and urged people to listen to what we had to say about Jesus.

After the greeting, I told the story of how God created the world perfectly, how humanity was separated from God by ignoring him and following their own desires, and how God provided a way back to him through Jesus's sacrificial death and resurrection.

Then, our Malian friend, Paul, stood before the crowd and shared his journey of faith in becoming a follower of Jesus. By that point, around 125 people sat before us. Because the crowd showed no signs of departing and we needed to leave the village the next day, Paul shared from the Bible late into the night. Following the teaching, several people approached us with their interest to know more, and we assured them a teacher would come back soon.

Over the next few years, Paul, I, and our friends from Mission 10:14 continued to visit Didiane. Ahmed was the first to follow Christ publicly. When many others professed their faith in Christ, the first baptisms took place in Didiane with seven new believers. Musa was thrilled. After decades of being the only Christian from his village, he now saw the fruit of his sacrifice. The journey has not been easy for Musa or the new believers in Didiane, but God is bringing fruit. Musa said, "I dreamed of this day. I knew I needed to endure hardship to open the doors for my village. I am amazed now because I see God is bringing my people into his light!"

Released from the Wassoulou

Ever since I had first moved into a Wassoulou village, I had felt a burden for the first Wassoulou churches to be started. Our family's move to New York City was linked to that burden. I took five trips to Mali during my first few years living in New York and spent about half of my time visiting Wassoulou villages. On that last trip, I thought back over the last decade and reflected on all God had done.

He had brought the Wassoulou church into existence. The first believers had come forth and were baptized in various villages. New laborers had been raised up from Mali and America to carry on the work of evangelism, discipleship, and church planting. The work among the Wassoulou was still just beginning, but even before I flew back from Mali to America on that last trip, I felt released from my decade-long burden. I felt God no longer wanted me to work among the Wassoulou.

That feeling was strange. I had finished my research and *ethNYcity* book and had more time to spend with West Africans. I had spent three to five weeks a year in Mali and dreamed of my family living several months of every year in Africa. My story throughout my whole working life intertwined with this remote Malian ethnic group. "Why would I be released from this work now?" I wondered. Ironically, my trips to Wassoulou land had become comfortable, routine, and even sacred.

When I become comfortable in anything, however, I often think of the Corrie Ten Boom quote: "I have learned to hold all things loosely, so God will not have to pry them out of my hands."[5] Through my regular prayers of seeking God's will, I knew he was removing from me the burden I had long felt for the Wassoulou. I needed to release the Wassoulou from my hands. On that last trip, I solemnly approached Paul the evangelist, Ahmed in Didiane, and the village chief of my adopted village Bandogo, and explained that I did not know if, or when, I would return. I explained that Mali was like a second home, they were special to me, and God had a way of keeping people connected.

My trip back to America was sad and somewhat lonely. I did not understand why God was diverting my efforts elsewhere, and I did not know where those efforts would be diverted. My time among the Wassoulou had been some of the most meaningful, faith growing, and fruitful in my life. And while the Lord had raised up other laborers among them, the needs were still great. But I periodically ask God, "What do I need to start doing?" and the even harder question, "What do I need to stop doing?" in order to seek what he desires instead of what seems right to me.

Our calling does not always have to make sense, but it is always to obey God and his path. I have learned enough in following God's Superplan to know he sometimes diverts us from particular vocations, activities, or locations that feel sacred, satisfying, or successful, to trust him into the unknown.

Part of living in God's Superplan is realizing we do not own, nor are we entitled to, anything. We are only stewards of possessions, relationships, and callings he entrusts to us. Sometimes the journey of God's Superplan requires us to release what we steward for reasons unknown. Few people have experienced such detours as much as Yusuf, whose story continues to unfold with twists of suffering and joy.

---

[1] Ntogoma told me once that his first son's only request from America was a Tupac Shakur shirt. Ntogoma struggled with how to respond because he was concerned about Tupac's influence on his child.

[2] *More than Dreams* is a series of five short movies that reenact true stories of Muslims coming to faith in Christ, with dreams of Jesus being one part of their journey. For more information, visit www.morethandreams.org.

[3] www.mission1014.org.

[4] Any West African who lives in New York is perceived to be wealthy.

[5] Corrie Ten Boom reportedly said variations of this quote often toward the end of her life. Another version says, "I must learn to hold earthly things lightly because if I do not the Lord might have to pry away my fingers, and that hurts." See Pam Rosewell Moore, *Life Lessons from the Hiding Place* (Grand Rapids: Chosen Books, 2004) 53.

Yusuf PART II

18

But seek first the kingdom of God and his righteousness, and all these things will be added to you (Matthew 6:33).

ONE YEAR AFTER YUSUF'S life-altering vision of Jesus in Burkina Faso, he was healthy, off the streets, and filled with purpose. He had obtained a respectable job teaching schoolchildren. He had become part of a church community. He had even saved enough money to buy a motorcycle.

One evening, while participating in an evangelism campaign with his church, Yusuf came across the same girl three times. Her name was Eunice, and her father was a Christian leader in the city. Over the next couple of years, Yusuf saw Eunice from time to time around town. When Eunice expressed interest in him, he told her, "You don't want to get close to me. I have a painful past, and you shouldn't share my pain. I'm supposed to live alone." But Eunice was willing to share the pain.

Marriages in Burkina Faso are family affairs in which the uniting of families is as central to the event as the couple's union. Yusuf's family no longer claimed him, and Eunice's family was not fond of their daughter marrying a man from a Muslim background without a family. Even on her wedding day, Eunice's family members questioned her. "Are you sure you want to do this? This is your choice. We are not responsible for what happens to you."

Jonathan, by now a respected and wealthy business owner, served in the traditional family role of vouching for the groom's character and pledging to support the couple. To Yusuf's surprise, his uncle also pledged his support, even hosting the marriage festivities in his home. This uncle (his mother's brother) had studied abroad in Europe, married a European, and felt disdain for his sister because of the way she had treated Yusuf. Even though the uncle was Muslim, he stepped foot in a church to represent Yusuf's family at the wedding ceremony. But the uncle's support poked the embers of malice within Yusuf's family, reigniting their desire to kill him. In their eyes, even more shame was brought upon them when Yusuf married a Christian.

The Motorcycle Incident

Months later, Yusuf heard that the elders in his family hired the men, but all he saw were outlines of two men walking in the middle of the road. It was an hour past midnight, two years after Yusuf's wedding, and he was returning home on his motorcycle from a late-night prayer meeting. As Yusuf neared the two men, they looked back to see him coming, made a sudden split to opposite sides of the road, and lifted a rope as Yusuf sped by. Yusuf tried to duck under the rope, but he was too late.

The next thing Yusuf remembers was waking up at 5:00 a.m. with the front end of his motorcycle pressed into the roadside concrete gutter. Yusuf had somehow remained partly on the bike, but his legs were wedged against the gutter's side. Yusuf surveyed his surroundings; the streets were empty. He was dizzy and in pain, but he managed to pull himself and the motorcycle out of the gutter and walked home. In the light of his living room, Yusuf looked down at his pants. He thought they were wet because of the gutter, but he now saw they were soaked in blood. Dizziness overtook him, and he passed out on the floor.

Yusuf's legs were bleeding in multiple places. Even today, scrape wounds bulge up and down Yusuf's legs, and indentations are visible where metal cylinders from the side of the gutter had gouged Yusuf's flesh. Yusuf had lost a lot of blood, and he was home alone because his wife Eunice was at a church retreat. When he regained consciousness, still early in the morning, Yusuf stumbled out the front door attempting to find a phone. But he passed out again on his doorstep. A mechanic shop was across the street, and a couple of men saw Yusuf's flailing body hit the ground. They ran over, picked him up, and rushed him to the hospital.

The doctors determined that Yusuf's blood loss caused him to pass out and, fortunately, there was no severe damage to his head. Eunice and Jonathan hurried to Yusuf's side at the hospital. Jonathan was crying, "They want to kill you! They want to kill you!" Eunice told Yusuf he needed to flee the country for his life.

After five days, the hospital released Yusuf, and a week later, Yusuf and Eunice's only child, Neema, was born. For the next three years, Eunice urged Yusuf, "You have to leave the country. You won't live long if you stay. I'd rather you be safe in another country than die in our own."

Yusuf had a steady job, a loving wife, a new child, a good church, and a lifelong friend in Jonathan. He did not want to leave Burkina Faso. But Yusuf and Eunice were constantly concealing their location and looking over their shoulder, wondering when the next attack would come. After thinking about escaping for two and a half years, Yusuf approached Jonathan.

"I think I need to leave the country."

Jonathan replied, "I thought the same thing, but I didn't want to say anything because of your wife and child. Where do you want to go? Paris? I have business contacts in Paris."

"No," Yusuf said. "I don't think so."

They committed this thought to prayer and one day Jonathan mentioned to Yusuf, "The United States is the safest place to go, but I don't know anyone in America."

"Neither do I," Yusuf said. But Eunice and Yusuf felt at peace with the idea of Yusuf escaping to the United States. Three years after the motorcycle incident, Yusuf visited the United States Embassy. "Where do you want to go?" they asked. Yusuf had not thought that far ahead, so he answered with the only place that came to mind—New York City. Within weeks, Yusuf boarded a plane to New York with a small suitcase, no money, and a telephone number he had somehow obtained of an unknown distant relative in New York.

Lost in New York

Yusuf was honest with the immigration official at JFK International Airport. "Where are you staying? Where are you going?" the official asked.

Yusuf replied, "I have no idea."

Yusuf's response earned him a trip to one of those side rooms where interrogations take place—the type with plain tables, chairs, and walls instead of welcome banners and videos of smiling, diverse Americans enjoying the nation's wonders. An officer entered the room and stared at Yusuf.

"Do you know anyone in the United States? Where do you plan to go?"

Yusuf mentioned his distant relative and showed the piece of paper with the scribbled phone number, but the number was incomplete. After further questioning, they decided Yusuf was harmless and allowed him to enter the country.

But Yusuf couldn't leave the airport. He proceeded to baggage claim, retrieved his suitcase, and stared past the sliding doors. Wind gusts spewed flaky white stuff off the ground in every direction, and the below-freezing temperatures made the wind's touch biting cold. In Burkina Faso, people wear scarves and jackets when the winter hits a frigid low of 62 degrees Fahrenheit (17 degrees Celsius). According to one list, Burkina Faso has the second-highest average temperature of any country in the world.[1] Yusuf arrived in New York wearing slacks and a thin sport coat. He did not own a jacket, and even inside baggage claim, his teeth chattered as he prayed for help.

Yusuf had no idea what to do. He had no money. His contact's phone number was incomplete. He was cold. And he was hungry. So, he sat in a chair in baggage claim and did nothing, save the few minutes of sleep he mustered between blasts of cold air from outside. After 10 hours in the airport, most of which was spent in the same chair, security guards approached Yusuf. They had been watching him on airport monitors. They questioned Yusuf and discovered he had no money and nowhere to go, so they threatened to send him back to his country. If not for a policeman's charity,

Yusuf might have returned to Burkina Faso in disgrace. One of the policemen spotted an African cab driver outside of baggage claim hustling for passengers. The policeman pulled a wad of cash out of his wallet and gave it to the cab driver with the following instructions: "Take this man to where his people are."

Yusuf was dropped off in Harlem's Little Africa, and he entered the same Farafina Coffee Shop I frequently visited. But with Yusuf moneyless and his baggage taking up space during peak hours, the employees told him to keep warm in the subway station and to return later. Yusuf returned at 2:00 a.m. as the workers prepared to close. When someone looked at the incomplete phone number of Yusuf's relative, they noticed the first digit was missing from a Manhattan area code. Yusuf tried the corrected number, and an African man named Boubacar answered. Being the middle of the night, Boubacar was groggy and suspicious. "Who are you? How did you get this number?"

It turned out that Yusuf's relative no longer lived in that apartment, but Boubacar knew the man. "Where are you?" Boubacar asked. Yusuf had no clue, so he handed the phone to someone nearby to answer. The phone was returned to Yusuf and Boubacar said, "You are lucky! New York is a massive city. Get up and walk outside. Look across the street and five floors up. Do you see a light? I'm looking at you from the window."

If someone had not provided the missing digit to the phone number, or if Boubacar had not answered, or if Yusuf had not been dropped directly across the street from his relative's old apartment in a city of more than 8 million people, he likely would have slept in a subway station his first night in the city. Boubacar took Yusuf in until he found another place to live, and Yusuf's distant relative connected with Yusuf, helping him find a job at a grocery store downtown. God was working out the details in his Superplan!

A Different Immigrant Narrative

When most immigrants arrive in New York City, especially if they are from one of the least-developed countries in the world,[2] they smell money and live for the American dream of wealth, achievement, and improving their quality of living. Indeed, Yusuf had escaped persecution in his home country for safety in America, but he began living for something, or Someone, in ways he had never done before. Yusuf explained, "I was in the wind, and God was taking me wherever he wanted me to go, and I did whatever he wanted me to do. He chose this life for me."

Within a week of arriving in New York, Yusuf asked his Muslim roommates about churches in the area. They did not have any suggestions, but as Yusuf walked around Harlem one day, he noticed a large church building (which happened to be the meeting place of the most evangelistic church in Harlem). Yusuf began sitting in the pews every time the church had a worship service or prayer meeting. "Church services became my English classes," Yusuf explained. With the aid of his church and job experience at the grocery store, Yusuf was having conversations in English within months.

Instead of filling his days off from work with second or third jobs (as is typical of Africans in New York), Yusuf joined his church's evangelism team. He had already been sharing the gospel at his workplace with West African co-workers, and two of those co-workers had experienced dramatic life change by turning from alcohol and drugs to Christ. One was a Muslim, the other a nominal Catholic. Yusuf, with his lowly status as a new immigrant, even had the nerve to share the gospel regularly with his employer. When Yusuf was told he needed to work Saturdays, instead of complying, as most immigrants would do, Yusuf replied:

I am sorry. I will work hard and extra time on the other days, but I cannot work on Saturdays. I devote Saturdays to God for evangelism. And I devote my Sundays to God for worship and community with other believers. I have made a covenant with God, not with you. Fire me if you want, but I cannot work on Saturdays.

Yusuf's boss responded the way downtown Manhattan bosses respond. "You can't tell me that! Who are you? This is not a church! You work when I tell you to work! I could replace you with another employee in minutes!"

Yusuf was almost fired on the spot, but the boss liked his honesty and work ethic and kept him employed. Yusuf's commitment and courage before his boss were rare. Usually, new arrivals from least-developed countries eagerly comply with employers because of their vulnerable economic status, acting somewhat like indentured servants. In many ways, immigrants (or many New Yorkers for that matter) become slaves to money. Yusuf, however, knew he had status that ranked higher than a downtown Manhattan boss—he was a child of God. And he was not afraid to appropriate that status if asked to compromise his role in God's Kingdom.

Yusuf's experience is strange because African immigrants (no matter what religion) typically feel as if their homeland is more spiritual and religious than New York. But Yusuf grabbed the freedom and opportunity in America not for money, but for becoming a minister, evangelist, and ambassador for God. He turned the American dream upside down, making bold choices to live in God's Superplan instead of floating in the New York current of materialism.

A few months after Yusuf and I met, the grocery store closed its doors, and Yusuf was without work. He had already contemplated devoting all his time to God in ministry, but he could not imagine how that choice would pay for his food and rent. When he read the words in Matthew 6:33, "Seek first the Kingdom of God and his righteousness, and all these things will be added to you," he was convinced he needed to give his life as service to God and trust him to provide for his needs.

From Curse to Freedom

Around one year before his job at the grocery store ended, Yusuf started a French-speaking prayer group that met in homes. I attended one of those meetings late that year. About 25 West African men and women squeezed onto couches, chairs, and every inch of floor they could find in a small living room. Another five to ten people, not finding space, sat in the hallway out of sight. Even though these men and women had busy schedules, they devoted around three hours one night a week to these meetings.

The group lifted their hearts to God in song and prayer. They interceded for one another, pleading with God for victory in their lives. They studied the Word of God, and they took care of each other's needs. They enjoyed talking and eating. The group members randomly provided food and drinks for each other. One person brought fried chicken, another brought rice and a large container of African sauce, and another brought sodas. Everyone had busy schedules and little sleep, but no one was eager to leave.

There are vibrant African Christian groups all over the city, so what happened in these meetings was not unique. Yusuf started pointing out to me, however, that many Christians from Muslim backgrounds attended the meetings.

"This one right here," Yusuf explained. "He is the son of an imam. He came to America and became an alcoholic. He has given his life to Christ and is cleaning up." Yusuf pointed out someone else from a Muslim-background, then another. Yusuf explained, "When we started this group, we wanted to focus on reaching Muslims from all over West Africa, not just gathering Christians from Burkina Faso."

Yusuf's purpose in starting the group is rare. In fact, I had never heard of another West African minister in the city who had done what Yusuf was doing. Usually, prayer groups and churches among immigrant groups are formed to help pre-existing Christians retain their faith and culture in the midst of their strange new environment. These groups become cultural fortresses to help members cling to their way of life; they are not formed for the missional or evangelistic motive of reaching others. But Yusuf's group was different.

I told Yusuf his group resembled the first church in the Book of Acts. "It looks like you are starting a church," I said. Shortly after, Yusuf formally started a church with his French-speaking group. They have over 150 people connected to their church today (including new groups they have started), but around 60 of these Christians come from Muslim-backgrounds—the largest number of Muslim-background believers in any church in Metro New York.

"In ministry to Muslims," Yusuf said, "we have to be patient. Sometimes people want results right away. If we don't want to labor, we won't be fruitful. The fruit only comes after suffering." Yusuf was well acquainted with suffering through his conversion and early Christian life, but the suffering Yusuf talks about involves deliberate choices to deny ourselves comforts and conveniences for the sake of Muslims' salvation. Yusuf regularly fasts and prays for Muslims, and his idea of fun is praying and doing the work of God.

Yusuf's cell phone rings constantly. Many of the calls are requests for prayer. And many of those requests are from Muslims.

One Muslim woman called recently saying a friend gave her Yusuf's phone number so he could pray for her. This woman had spent over a year's wages on sorcerers to cure her health issues. Through Yusuf and the French-speaking church, she was delivered of these ailments by Jesus within a week's time, gave her life to Christ, and began testifying of Jesus's power and identity to the sorcerers who could not heal her.

Many West African Muslims live in a world where sorcery and the spiritual world affect daily life. They regularly perform sacrifices and wear amulets to seek protection from evil spirits. Many of them are cursed by family members or neighbors. Some of them are cursed because they, or their ancestors, have made pacts with evil spirits. No matter what one believes about evil spirits at work in the world, the curse of death because of sin affects West African Muslims and all people without Christ.[3]

Yusuf addresses these issues by praying for people's release from curses, but explains that freedom from curses can only come through Jesus Christ. He has seen God use the power of prayer to open Muslims' eyes to the truth and power of God's Word.[4] Around half of the people attending the church's Friday night prayer meetings are Christians from Muslim backgrounds—and some people attend who are still Muslim. The Friday night prayer meetings have proven more effective at gathering Muslims to hear the gospel of Jesus than the Sunday worship services. Muslims feel a need for prayer and power, and Yusuf teaches them the power of Jesus and his message from the Bible.

Yusuf's kindness is so well known in the Muslim community that when some Muslims hear of new arrivals in America or people in need, they refer them to "the pastor" instead of the mosque. One Muslim man from Burkina Faso showed up recently on Yusuf's doorstep because a Muslim compatriot passed on Yusuf's address. This man was overwhelmed by the love of Christians and gave his life to Christ within his first few weeks in America.

Yusuf laughed in astonishment at how God is using him in America. He said:

> *Can you believe this? I was never involved in ministry back home. I come from a poor country. When I came to America, I had nothing, and I knew no one.*

*I haven't worked for a paycheck for nine years. But I even have wealthy white
people asking me to pray for them now! I think sometimes, how did I get here?
I just try to live by faith and obey God. That's it!*

One irony in Yusuf's journey is that his limited job opportunities
in America pushed him further into ministry. "If jobs had come
easier," Yusuf said, "maybe I wouldn't have immersed myself in
ministry to the point where I couldn't do anything else. I was in the
wind, and God took me places."

Through Yusuf's activity in God's Superplan, people have been
healed and delivered from demonic oppression, addictions, and
sin. Dozens of people have given their lives to Christ. Godly marriages have begun. Churches and prayer groups have been birthed
to witness to their communities. New Muslim-background Christians have shared their testimonies and the gospel of Jesus Christ
with their contacts back home, and some of those have given their
lives to Christ. The witness of the new church has spread back to
Africa and through the African diaspora worldwide.

Yusuf reflected on his adventure with God:

*Adventures are adventures because they're unpredictable. Sometimes crazy and
unpredictable events take place. Sometimes the adventure isn't comfortable. Sometimes you don't know how things are going to turn out. People see results in our
ministry now, but they don't see all the sacrifice put into it. I believe obeying
God's leading, even when his leading doesn't make much sense, is why I see
fruit in my life.*

Yusuf's spirit-filled life may seem extraordinary. One must remember, however, how far Yusuf has come. At one point as a Christian, he was homeless, lived an unhealthy lifestyle, and was about
to revert to Islam, kill himself, or go crazy. No one is too far gone.
Yusuf's character and fruitfulness can only be understood through
decades of God's work in shaping his life and role in the Superplan.
Yusuf is an ordinary person who still has deep pains and struggles,
but he has chosen not to let those struggles control or define him.

Yusuf often reflects upon Isaiah 10:15, "Shall the ax boast over
him who hews with it, or the saw magnify itself against him who
wields it? As if a rod should wield him who lifts it, or as if a staff
should lift him who is not wood!"

"We are nothing," Yusuf explained. "I am not talking about those Christians who live for money and status. I am talking about those who live for God's plan—those who go on the adventure with him. We are just ambassadors. We are in the wind, and he takes us where he desires."

[1] Nikola Potrebic, "11 Countries with Highest Average Temperatures in the World," *Insider Monkey*, 26 Oct. 2015, www.insidermonkey.com/blog/11-countries-with-highest-average-temperature-in-the-world-378565/, Accessed 22 Sep. 2016.

[2] Burkina Faso is the third least-developed country in the world, and it has ranked around that number for as long as these lists have existed. See "About Least-Developed Countries," UN-OHRLLS, n.d., unohrlls.org/about-ldcs/, Accessed 24 Sep. 2016.

[3] "For all who rely on works of the law are under a curse; for it is written, 'Cursed be everyone who does not abide by all things written in the Book of the Law, and do them'" (Galatians 3:10). "For as by a man came death, by a man has come also the resurrection of the dead. For as in Adam all die, so also in Christ shall all be made alive" (1 Corinthians 15:21-22).

[4] Yusuf and I worked on a presentation of the gospel based on Yusuf's experiences with leading Muslims to Christ through prayer and explaining Christ's role in freeing people from the curse of sin "by becoming a curse for us" (Gal 3:13). View a short video presentation of the "3 Circles Curse" at vimeo.com/158980913. You can view an outline of a longer Curse Story presentation at "The Curse Story," *Global Gates*, 9 May 2015, globalgatesinfo.wordpress.com/2015/05/09/72/, Accessed 14 Apr. 2017.

> There is no fear in love, but perfect love casts out
> fear. For fear has to do with punishment, and
> whoever fears has not been perfected in love. We
> love because he first loved us (1 John 4:18-19).

FEAR IS THE MOST difficult barrier for people to overcome in sharing the gospel. I do not know an easy way to push past fear. People can remind themselves repeatedly to cast anxieties on the Lord, but doing so sometimes accomplishes nothing more than perpetuating fearful thoughts. A practical way to cast anxiety on the Lord is to take the plunge of faith to do what one fears. I still sometimes get anxious and feel out of place when I step into a Muslim's world. But the more steps of faith I take, the more my anxiety lessens and the more the Lord helps me overcome my fear. What a tragedy it is when I refuse to share my life and the gospel with Muslims or others because of my fear. Below are three examples of when I actually moved past anxiety, took risks, and stepped into Muslims' space to share my life and the message of Jesus.

Dancing White Man

I should have known. The previous time I attended a West African concert in the Bronx, the organizers said the event began at 9:30 p.m. Tipped off by insiders that the starting time was always a couple of hours after the published time, I arrived at 11:00 p.m. Even though it was a Thursday night and most people had to work the next day, the musicians sauntered onto the stage at 1:30 a.m. I stayed for three songs and left.

Years later, a West African fundraising concert I planned to attend was supposed to be different. One of the event organizers was a Malian women's association leader named Katy. She insisted I attend the concert to give a short speech in support of the concert's cause, which was raising awareness and funds for women's development programs in Mali. I gave a skeptical look when she mentioned a 9:00 p.m. start, but she and her husband insisted the concert would begin on time. Still skeptical, I arrived with Yusuf at 10:00 p.m. We were not skeptical enough because the concert didn't begin until 1:30 a.m.

When the big daddies and mommas in the Malian diaspora attended a function together, the event was newsworthy in Mali. The Malian national television station sent a crew to film and host the event, and the concert was later shown on primetime television in Mali. The concert had much pageantry, with dignitaries and honored guests giving flowery speeches in between every song or two.

At 3:00 a.m., I was fading fast and longing for bed, which was 45 minutes away. The concert didn't have an end in sight, and I had never been called upon to speak to the crowd. Yusuf and I decided to leave. As we gathered our belongings, however, Katy's husband tapped me on the shoulder and ushered me to meet the event's emcee.

Within minutes, I was called to the front to not only speak to over 200 concert attendees, but also to all of Mali through the country's one television station! As I reached for the microphone, the emcee stepped back and demanded, "Oh, before you speak, you have to dance!"

I told her she was funny and said, "Oh, my sister, you must not know because you just arrived in America, but white men can't dance!" I reached for the microphone again while she laughed, but she stepped back and insisted, "Dance."

She wouldn't budge. With cameras rolling and out of options, I rapidly shuffled my feet and flung my arms in my best imitation of a Malian dance. I know I looked like a fool, so I figured a 30-second dance was enough embarrassment to earn the microphone. I was wrong. The emcee insisted I dance longer. "Five minutes," she said. I started up again and, thankfully, Katy and others came to my rescue by dancing alongside me. After a few minutes, I finally satisfied the emcee's appetite for watching a dancing white man, and she relinquished the microphone.

I was already laughing inside at what God has his people sometimes do to share his Word. I took the microphone and shared some wisdom gleaned from God's Word. I said:

> *It is easy for us to look at what other people possess and insist they give us some of what they own or know. But God has entrusted all of us with different possessions and gifts. If we cannot first work with what God has entrusted to us, why would God entrust us with anything more? Instead, work with that which God has entrusted to you. If he finds you faithful in these small things, God will entrust larger things to you, and he himself will lift you up.*

Apparently, the words were well received. A joyous eruption burst forth from the audience unlike any other at the concert. A famous traditional Malian singer came forward to sing blessings over me. Within minutes, a dozen people or so danced around me, lifted up my hands, stuffed wads of cash into the singer's hands, and laughed away at the spectacle. When dozens of women broke out in a conga-line celebration for 10 minutes, I slowly removed myself from the chaos. I mingled with the crowd at the back a bit and made a 3:45 a.m. journey back home.

A few days later, I visited a Malian family. One of the women had attended the concert and told me how great my dancing had been.

"It wasn't great," I said. "I can't dance at all. I made a fool of myself! It was like someone took a fish out of the water and threw it on dry land. I danced like a flopping fish!"

My transparency helped the woman express her true feelings. "Oh no, Mamadou, it was nothing like that! Your dancing was more like the sight of a chicken running around a courtyard, right after its head is cut off!"

Wow! For the next few years, I received comments from people all over America and Mali who had seen me dance. Malian television repeatedly showed the concert. An official DVD was released of the event, which included captions commenting on my dancing skills.

Dancing at the event was uncomfortable, but I prayed God used my words to draw people to himself and his Word. I had been given an opportunity to share wisdom from God's Word to a predominantly Muslim country on national television!

A couple of years after the concert, I came across a Malian Muslim couple. The woman said, "I have wanted to see you ever since that event. I still remember the words you spoke. I think about them all the time, and I've tried to apply that wisdom in how I approach helping people in my country." Shortly after, a Bible study began in her home.

Second Naming Ceremony

Three years after our first daughter was born, our third child, another daughter, inhaled New York air for the first time. Since our first naming ceremony was well received and meaningful, we decided to hold a similar ceremony. This time, however, we avoided the inevitable half-eaten lamb in our child's crib by holding the event in a Muslim-run center. The center usually leased their space at a premium rate, but they gave us the room for free since we provided English classes and other services for the community.

A year or two earlier, when we began teaching English at the center, an association leader named Keita pulled me into his office. He said, "Mamadou, everyone is busy in New York City. Why do you take the time to provide services for our community?"

Keita was a devout Muslim and a gatekeeper for his community, and even though I had explained who we were and why we had started the class to other leaders, Keita had not made up his mind about approving our presence. I explained to Keita that I could never be as good of a host as West Africans were to me in their countries, but I wanted to return hospitality. I continued, "We are also followers of Jesus. And as I have studied the life of Jesus and looked at his example, I see that he loved others and gave his life for them. Yes, we could spend our time in the city making money or entertaining ourselves, but we want to follow Jesus's example."

Keita gave an approving smile. We developed a strong relationship from that point forward, not shying away from sharing our beliefs, but doing so with mutual respect. We invited Keita and others from the association to the naming ceremony. We invited West African leaders, English class students, and other friends we had made in the community. We also invited Yusuf back to conduct the ceremony as our "Christian imam."

Over 60 people crammed into the building for the event. As we had done before, we shared the joyous occasion of our child's birth by adopting the form of an African Muslim event and transforming it to honor Jesus. Of course, the difference between this ceremony and the last was the setting; this one was held in a Muslim-run center! Nevertheless, after Yusuf announced the name of the child to the crowd, I shared how a woman, over 100 years ago, followed God's leading to India and rescued girls from forced prostitution in temples. Her life of caring for others and teaching people God's Word, I explained, inspired us to name our child after her.

Yusuf then shared the message of salvation through Jesus, held up our child, and prayed God's blessing over her. When Yusuf finished, I thanked everyone for coming, prayed over our feast of guinea fowl, fish, lamb, and plantains, and gave everyone the gift of a *JESUS* film DVD in their language.[1] Upon receiving the gift, the crowd broke out in applause, thanking us for the DVD and shouting blessings to our daughter and family.

One Muslim woman said, "The words you all spoke were good speech. The message you shared is true." One man picked up on the woman's words. "Yes, you're right. It's true. We might just convert!" But the tone and laughter in his voice revealed the impossibility in his mind of such a change. One Muslim man, however, stood in the back of the room and yelled a blessing, "May your child do greater things in our country than that woman did in India!"

Such a blessing capped off a beautiful ironic evening. During a Christian naming ceremony held in a Muslim-run center and mainly attended by Muslims, a Muslim man gave a blessing for our daughter to do greater things in his Muslim country than the Christian missionary she was named after had done in India. I could only say in response, "Amen. May God grab on to the blessing."

The Mosque

One day while talking to Keita, he mentioned he had helped start a new mosque and encouraged me to meet the imam. "He's open-minded," Keita said. "He's not like some of the others."

On one of my weekly visits with Yusuf, we decided to walk into the mosque to see if the imam was available. We entered through the men's doorway, slipped off our shoes, and greeted the men nearby. A regal-looking man with a pointy beard, glasses, and long-flowing African robe sat with an Arabic-scripted book across the room. The man looked up from his reading and beckoned us toward him. We greeted, and I explained that my friend Keita had urged me to visit the new mosque to meet the imam.

"Welcome," the man said. "My name is Bakary. I am the imam here. Keita is a good man, and he has also told me about you. I was looking forward to meeting you. He says you are a good person who has helped our community."

Yusuf, Bakary, and I chatted for a while, then Bakary asked, "So what were you doing in Mali?"

There are multiple ways to answer that question, especially on the first visit with an imam in a mosque, but I felt compelled to share how Jesus called me away from a comfortable life to follow him. I shared a short story of the Bible's message from Creation to Christ. I explained that the hope and promise of Paradise we have in Jesus was worth dying for, and that I almost experienced that firsthand in Mali. Bakary listened intently without feeling a need to defend his Islamic beliefs. He thanked me for sharing, and before we left, Bakary urged Yusuf and me to return for conversation.

A few months later, Keita informed me of the opportunity to teach English at the mosque through a city program. Because we had experienced a positive meeting with Bakary, I decided to become certified with the city to teach their English program in the mosque. The city program only lasted two months, but it was well received. Around 15 men and women attended these meetings. After one of the first meetings, Bakary pulled me aside and said, "I want you to teach me the Bible." I had not spoken about the Bible in the mosque since I first met Bakary, so I was surprised at his words. "Okay," I answered. "We can do that!"

Bakary and I began studying the Bible almost every week in the mosque. He was not afraid to let people know what he was studying, and I noticed on many occasions people stopped what they were doing to listen to our conversation. As the city's English program neared an end, I took a risk to see if Bakary would allow me to continue English classes in the mosque, but by teaching the Bible. He thought for a moment, but answered, "No, I can't let you teach the Bible here. You can teach me, but I can't let you openly teach the Bible in the mosque."

"Okay," I said. "Can I carry on the English classes teaching character and values?"

"Of course," Bakary replied.

And thus began, as a follower of Christ, my role as a shaper of morality in a Muslim mosque. I took topics such as "honesty," and spent one to three lessons on each topic, teaching English and shaping morality simultaneously. Although I was not given permission to teach the Bible, the group felt in some ways like a discipleship group. We had great discussions about morality and how to apply the teaching to specific situations in our life, and we encouraged one another in making virtuous choices.

One evening, a man who had attended a few English classes greeted the group. "Are you going to join us tonight?" I asked.

"No!" he said. "I am going to pray and learn Arabic tonight! On the Day of Judgment, Allah is not going to ask me if I learned English. He's going to ask me if I learned Arabic!" Then he stormed off.

I looked around at the English students. Some had no reaction. Some expressed disgust at the man's words. One student vocalized his disgust, saying, "You hear these Muslims? They are so fanatical sometimes. He thinks that Allah is going to ask him if he learned Arabic on the Day of Judgment! He's crazy!"

Any time a Muslim man uses the phrase, "these Muslims," it grabs my attention. Later that night, I walked out of the mosque with the man who said those words. "Talk to me more about what you were thinking earlier," I said. When he continued to express disgust toward some Muslims' beliefs, I walked with him away from the mosque to carry on our conversation. That night, he agreed he wanted to begin studying the Bible. How would I have found that guy if I had not been present in the mosque to watch these events play out?

I became a regular at the mosque. When they prayed, I sat to the side and prayed silently for those in the room. The mosque leaders were so comfortable with my presence that they sometimes left me in the mosque alone when I was waiting for someone. One day a mosque leader said, "Hey, do you want the Wi-Fi code? We don't give the code out to people in the mosque, but we will give it to you." I lived in the strange reality that I had more access to a mosque than I had to any church building in the city. The mosque leaders might have even given me keys to the building if I had asked for them.

Before one of my Bible studies began with Bakary, he brought up the elephant in the room. "Do you know why we allow you here in the mosque?" he asked.

"Actually, no, I don't. Why?"

"Look," he said. "Everyone here knows you are a Christian and some know you are a pastor. But you respect us and love us, and everyone here loves you. You are part of our community, and we love having you here."

I felt welcomed and at home, even though everyone knew I was different. What if churches made Muslims feel the same way? To this day, Bakary claims he studies the Bible every day. We studied the Bible in the mosque for a couple of years before he moved away. These studies were so frequent that another imam became jealous and asked that I study the Bible with him.

That second imam is the one who told me later:

I have had Christians try to give me a Bible before. I told them, "I do not have time for that. I am an imam and cannot have your book near me. I need to be in the Qur'an." I have realized this is a mistake. I did not know about Christians. We Muslims say we know all the prophets. We say we know Jesus. But all that we know about him is in the Qur'an. We cannot know Jesus if we do not love him, and I realize now we cannot know Jesus or love him if we do not know the Bible. Today has done something to me. I am happy inside. I have to know the Bible.

This imam continues to show his words weren't empty.

One never knows what waits behind a mosque door. Thankfully, Yusuf and I walked through the door that day. Meanwhile, there was another door of opportunity our family could not ignore, but walking through it was difficult because doing so meant turning away from the door we had long been walking toward.

---

[1] You can view and purchase multi-language *JESUS* film DVDs, featuring the languages most spoken by immigrants, from *Reaching the Nations Among Us*, www.reachingthenationsamongus.org.

Gateways

> *And he made from one man every nation of mankind to live on all the face of the earth, having determined allotted periods and the boundaries of their dwelling place, that they should seek God, and perhaps feel their way toward him and find him. Yet he is actually not far from each one of us (Acts 17:26-27).*

THE CITY IS STRESSFUL on families. Before we started homeschooling, our first two children were fortunate enough to attend one of Harlem's best public schools. But even though we only lived a mile from the school, we spent three hours a day commuting and waiting for children. Snow and its sludgy aftermath posed even more challenges for our walking commute. A drop-off at the same distance in the suburbs would have taken five minutes by car.

Our second apartment, which seemed spectacular after our first apartment experience, ended up harming our children's health. Our first month in the Little Africa apartment, a repairman forgot to patch a hole in the roof, and a torrential rain brought gushing water into our closet. Management was slow to respond and mold developed. Eventually, however, they came and "fixed the problem."

Our family had throat and upper respiratory issues the next two and a half years. Even though our son was treated for asthma by the age of three, we didn't recognize the source of our problems because our symptoms were normally mild. One day, however, our son had difficulty breathing and was rushed to the pediatrician. When he did not respond to breathing treatments, the pediatrician called an emergency ambulance. Thankfully, he started breathing normally, and the ambulance was called off, but he was diagnosed with pneumonia. During the same week, our 11-month-old daughter's breathing went into distress. An ambulance rushed her to the hospital where she was diagnosed with bronchitis. She recovered well, but when the doctors heard about our ongoing respiratory issues, they advised us to check for mold.

Knowing our management would not pay the fee, we spent several hundred dollars for a mold inspection which revealed black mold and two other types of toxic mold in the "fixed" closet. The level of toxic mold in our apartment was 1,000 times the recommended safe level.

The mold inspector spoke to us sternly. "If this were my family," he said, "I would not stay in the apartment one more night."

Silly us! We figured if we showed management the dangerous toxic mold levels in our building and explained how we were hospitalized as a result, they would quickly remedy the problem. Instead, the managers feared a lawsuit, screamed at us on the phone, gave us an eviction notice, and threatened to sue us for harassment because we insisted they remove the mold for the next tenant.

We were forced to find a new apartment within days, but the most affordable home we found was in a worse part of Harlem on the sixth floor without an elevator.[1] About a year after moving, we discovered Nichole was pregnant with our third child. Faced with having three small children and six floors to ascend and descend, we laid down half of our life savings as a down payment deposit to purchase a co-op apartment with an elevator.[2]

But the transaction took place after America's mortgage crisis. A new government stipulation affected loans for our particular co-op building. When the lender became aware of the new law, they were unable to give us a loan. Our bank had offered needed down payment assistance, and no other lender offered the same perk, so we backed out of the deal. Instead of returning our money, the co-op kept it, claiming the money belonged to them because of fine print in our contract. We were forced to either go to court with an undetermined outcome and thousands of dollars in lawyer fees or settle out of court. Two years passed before we reached a settlement, so we remained in our sixth-floor apartment until better housing opened up in the Bronx.

Most people leave their mission field because of living issues, not because of problems with the people they work among.[3] Several years passed before Nichole felt at home in the city. But something changed over time. God transformed Nichole's view of the city, and she persevered through tough living situations. She jokes about writing a book called, "How Harlem Killed Me and Why That's a Good Thing," to share lessons learned about dying to herself to live for God's plans.[4]

Three to four years after we moved to Harlem, we were in a taxi coming from LaGuardia Airport after an out-of-town trip. I still remember the look on Nichole's face as we crossed the Triborough Bridge and faced the Manhattan skyline. Her face beamed as she said, "We're home. New York City is home. We're going home." It was the first time she said those words. And Harlem is now her favorite neighborhood.

Our original plan was to live in New York City for two to three years then move to Africa. When I finished *ethNYcity*, our family was able to re-assess our calling and locale, and a move to Mali or Paris was enticing. Nichole had never lived in one city for more than four years until New York! But as we prayed, reflected, and talked about opportunities, we could not ignore what we had learned from four years of ministry and research in New York City.

Reaching the Nations Through New York City

I did not know the significance of Metro New York for pioneer missions until we did our research. If the members of unreached people groups in Metro New York were counted as a city, that unreached city would have a larger population than Los Angeles.[5] Linguists estimate around 800 languages are spoken in New York City.[6] Up to two-thirds of the city's population were born in another country or are children of people born elsewhere.

The metropolitan area of New York has a population of over 20 million. Two million of those are Jews. While there are a large number of American and Israeli Jews, significant Jewish populations hail from unexpected places like Morocco, Syria, Lebanon, Uzbekistan, Russia, Egypt, Yemen, and Afghanistan. There are dozens of Hasidic Jewish communities, not only in Yiddish-speaking city neighborhoods, but also in their own suburban villages featuring dress codes and esoteric customs.[7]

There are around one million Muslims in the metropolitan area from countries like Senegal, Bangladesh, Pakistan, Afghanistan, Egypt, India, Syria, Yemen, Turkey, Albania, and Iran.[8] There are also around 500,000 Hindus and 80,000 Sikhs. The numbers were staggering to me, especially since some immigrants in Metro New York come from areas with little or no exposure to the life and message of Jesus.

Yemen, for instance, has one of the smallest Christian populations of any country in the world, and in the last decade, most American missionaries in Yemen have either lost their ability to remain in the country or have been killed. My family had access to Yemen, however, by buying a sandwich. Yemeni men own most of the delis in Harlem while their families often remain in Yemen. One deli owner talked about us to his wife back home, and Nichole frequently greeted her on the phone. He sent our family's picture back home, and his wife sent traditional clothing to Nichole as a gift. Our smiling faces might be on display in a house in Yemen somewhere!

Many people have the view, undoubtedly aided by the secular media, that New York City's residents are uninterested in religion. Because of an influx of religious immigrants, however, this view is inaccurate. New York City has transformed over the last few decades into a post-secular existence—one in which religious adherence and devotion is normative for the average New Yorker. And the influx of religious immigrants is not only taking place in major urban areas like New York. Refugees, in particular, are placed in smaller cities and towns with an abundance of cheap housing.

While research on unreached peoples in North America is ongoing, the United States may have the most diverse representation of unreached people groups in the world.[9] Even though Nichole and I were, at first, reluctant missionaries in America, we had stumbled into the most strategic city in the most strategic country in the world to engage the world's least-reached people groups with the message of Jesus.

There was little zeal or passion for missions in New York City. I had come from areas of the United States where churches had missions ministers on staff to educate and involve their members in work among unreached people groups. Such efforts were rare in New York City churches. Perhaps people were too busy in New York, or churches struggled with devoting resources to something other than their survival or meeting social needs in their communities, but churches lacked intentional engagement with unreached peoples.

I also noticed that workers among unreached peoples in Metro New York were either from the people group they were trying to reach or were cross-cultural missionaries trained overseas who returned for health or family reasons (myself included). I could count on one hand the workers who did not have overseas experience, saw a need among unreached peoples in the city, and began devoting significant time to reach them. I knew we needed to raise up more trained laborers in our context.

Through our experience with Musa and other West Africans, we had seen how places like New York City were strategic gateways to reaching some of the world's least-reached peoples and places. Our relationships in New York grafted us into family relationships in Mali that we could not have experienced otherwise. These relational opportunities were not limited to Malians or the City of New York. Large numbers of unreached peoples from all over the world are bridging their lives into the culture of global gateway cities, where Christ-followers can reach them.

Edward Judson, a New York City pastor and son of America's first foreign missionary, Adoniram Judson, observed most eloquently in 1914:

> *Indeed, I am often thrilled by the thought that the long, healing shadow of my father's life touches City Missions and falls upon the foreigners that come in such vast throngs from the ends of the earth to settle in our great cities. We used to think of them as a menace, but have learned to regard them as an opportunity. It would seem as if our heavenly Father, perceiving that we Christians of America were so vitally interested in foreign races as to send our best men and women to them with the gospel, paying their traveling expenses and maintenance, deemed it wise to put in the hearts of the heathen to come from all parts of the world to our shores, paying their own expenses.*[10]

Judson made those remarks over 100 years ago at a time when the immigrant population in the United States did not yet include the variety of unreached people groups we have today. But even then, Judson recognized what eludes many: People who don't know Christ are paying their own expenses to travel to cities with large numbers of Christians, relating to new people by learning the host language and culture, and making it more natural and accessible for Christ-followers to share the hope that lies within them. Because unreached people groups only began mass migrating to urban areas in the past few decades, only recently have many churches, mission boards, and denominations begun outreach efforts to immigrants.

A New Horizon

When I was in Mali, I had great examples to follow with mission work among unreached people groups in villages. But in America, there are few examples to follow in reaching unreached diaspora peoples in gateway cities. As a result, I have felt like more of a pioneer missionary in New York than when I was the only missionary living among the unreached Wassoulou in Mali.

Nichole and I love the African village. But knowing the opportunities in New York City and the platform we had through our ministry and research to recruit more workers, we knew the next step in our journey with God was staying in the city, continuing to love West Africans but also helping others launch efforts among different unreached people groups. We had no idea what that would look like. Although we had not expected to live in New York for more than a few years, we knew we needed to respond to God's ushering the world into our city. After all, in most cases, we were still the only Christians someone knew.

But Muslims, Hindus, Sikhs, Jews, and Buddhists weren't the only religious immigrants moving to New York. Many of these immigrants were Christians. And some of these, like Yusuf, exchanged the pursuit of America's wealth and comforts for a continued adventure of suffering and joy in sharing the gospel with their people. God has been sending immigrant missionaries to America, and these are often the most fruitful laborers among unreached peoples in our cities. Aslam, a Christian who left Bangladesh for his family's safety, exemplifies someone whose witness has been emboldened within the freedom of America.

¹ For some reason, many people who visited counted the steps of our stairs. There were 82. People joked that our stairs were going to kill someone until they almost did. My dad had a stroke about halfway up. Thankfully, he recovered well.

² New York has its own real estate rules and customs. One common practice is the buyer has to put down a large amount of money as a deposit before the actual closing.

³ Spiritual warfare is often in the background of these issues with pioneer missionary workers.

⁴ Colossians 3:3-4 puts it this way, "Set your minds on things that are above, not on things that are on earth. For you have died, and your life is hidden with Christ in God."

⁵ I am referring to the population within the city limits of Los Angeles, which numbers under four million.

⁶ See Endangered Language Alliance (www.elalliance.org) or view Sam Roberts, "Listening to (and Saving) the World's Lost Languages," *New York Times*, 29 Apr. 2010, www.nytimes.com/2010/04/29/nyregion/29lost.html?_r=0, Accessed 12 Oct. 2016.

⁷ Kyrias Joel has a population of over 20,000 Hasidic Jews, mainly Satmar. The village is located in Monroe, NY, but Kyrias Joel leaders are actively seeking to create a separate town. Their village is already separate enough to include a welcoming sign that urges visitors to comply with their values. See "Welcome to Kyrias Joel: Please Dress Accordingly," *CBS New York*, 31 Aug. 2010, newyork.cbslocal.com/2010/08/31/welcome-to-kiryas-joel-please-dress-accordingly/, Accessed 12 Oct. 2016.

⁸ For population estimates and locales of specific Muslim peoples in Metro New York, view a nine-part-blog series starting with Chris Clayman, "Muslims in Metro New York (Part 1)," *Global Gates*, 22 Feb. 2016, globalgatesinfo. wordpress.com/2016/02/22/muslims-in-metro-new-york-part-1-one-million-muslims/, Accessed 16 Oct. 2016.

⁹ This statement might seem staggering, but one must remember that the United States receives around 20% of the world's immigrants—more than any other country. A significant minority of these immigrants are from unreached people groups. See J.D. Payne, *Unreached Peoples, Least Reached Places: An Untold Story of Lostness in America* (J.D. Payne, 2014) 29, www.jdpayne. org/wp-content/uploads/2014/02/Unreached-Peoples-Least-Reached-Places-Payne.pdf, Accessed 12 Oct. 2016. Also see J.D. Payne, "The Number of Unreached People Groups in the U.S. and Canada," *Missiologically Thinking*, 12 Apr. 2011, www.jdpayne.org/2011/04/12/the-number-of-unreached-people-groups-in-the-u-s-and-canada-a-call-for-more-and-better-urban-research-part-5/, Accessed 12 Oct. 2016.

¹⁰ Edward Judson, "Address," in *The Judson Centennial: 1814–1914*, eds. Howard B. Grose and Fred P. Haggard (Philadelphia: The American Baptist Publication Society, 1914), 157.

aslam 21

*Any one of you who does not renounce all that
he has cannot be my disciple (Luke 14:33).*

EARLY ON IN OUR time in New York City, I received a strange call
from a local Christian leader.

"Would you be willing to disciple four Bangladeshis from Muslim backgrounds in Queens?" the leader asked.

"Why are you asking me?" I replied. "I don't know much about
Bangladeshis. Beyond basic research, all my experience has been
with West Africans. And I live an hour away!"

"Well, four Bangladeshi Muslims expressed faith in Christ and
connected with a Bangladeshi church of Christian-background
people. Even though they are from the same country, the Christians struggle relating to them and discipling them. I thought you
could help."

Even though I was willing to help, the church did not want the
men influenced by outsiders. The church didn't disciple them, however, and I heard the Muslim-background Bangladeshis left the city
with only a nominal faith in Christ. I wonder if the story would have
changed with trained workers closer to the situation geographically
and culturally.

After we decided to stay in New York, the current of God's guidance led me to become more of a Barnabas than a Paul, in part
to address situations like that with the Bangladeshis. I had always
thought of a missionary as someone like Paul—sharing Christ on

the frontier instead of on foundations laid by someone else (Romans 15:20). But there was only a Paul as we know him because of Barnabas.

Acts 11 relates the story of a movement of God that emerged outside the mainstream Jewish-Christian community of the time. In Antioch, a growing number of Gentiles (non-Jews) were embracing Christianity. The Jerusalem church heard about this Gentile movement and sent Barnabas to check it out. With his credentials, knowledge, and experience, Barnabas could have remained in Antioch as its key leader. Instead, Barnabas recruited a diaspora Jew with Roman citizenship from Tarsus named Paul (who had limited contact with the Jerusalem church) and took him to Antioch to disciple the new believers. Later, this same Antioch church sent out Paul and Barnabas to experience the incredible feats recorded in the Book of Acts. Without Barnabas recruiting and encouraging Paul—who had the calling, gifting, and cultural background for effective ministry among the unreached peoples of the time—Christian history, and perhaps our own history, would have been drastically different.

With the diversity of needs among the unreached peoples of Metro New York, I needed to spend more time away from the frontlines to find Pauls, as well as other Barnabases, so that better options existed than I am (and I was rarely a good option!) to disciple people like those Bangladeshi men. Specifically with Bangladeshis, God brought a man named Brad to New York City as a Barnabas. Brad and his family had spent close to a decade in Asia as missionaries before God led them to Queens. As Brad surveyed the area, he knew Paul-type figures were needed among Bangladeshis, Pakistanis, and Indians, and he began to pray for those laborers.

Within a short time, Brad met a man named Aslam, a Bangladeshi Christian from a Muslim background who had recently arrived in New York City. Brad encouraged Aslam in his walk with the Lord and his witness among Bangladeshi Muslims. "Brad helped me so much," Aslam said, "to desire God more." With Brad and others by his side, Aslam became an effective missionary among Muslims in Metro New York. Like Yusuf, however, Aslam's current ministry cannot be fully appreciated without hearing his story.

A Mother's Silent Witness

Aslam grew up in a village of 7,000 people in the Chittagong district of Bangladesh. He said:

> *We lived in a box. There was no electricity in my village, no television, no Internet. Our village had many Muslims committed to whatever the Muslim gurus told them. Our area was known for radical Islam; it was a center for a violent political group that wanted Sharia law. I grew up thinking people from other religions were infidels, and we had no connection with Christians.*

By age six, every day before school and on the weekends, Aslam recited the Qur'an for an hour in Arabic. By age seven, he prayed the Muslim ritual prayers five times a day. Because Aslam's grandfather held a prominent position in society, visiting imams stayed in their home during the fasting month of Ramadan. These scholars taught Aslam and his siblings their knowledge of the Qur'an and the Islamic traditions. Many of Aslam's uncles and other family members made the hajj to Mecca, which deepened the family's roots in Islam.

Aslam continued his morning Qur'an recitals until he was a teenager. Life became more complicated at that point. His family was prominent in their society. Everyone was educated; many of his aunts and uncles were teachers. His mom tutored him in the evenings, and Aslam's dad had a respectable job at a railway station. But when Aslam was 16, his father abruptly quit his job and forced the family to live off savings. Those savings did not last long, and Aslam's father left to pursue riches in Saudi Arabia. As the eldest child, Aslam was expected to provide for his family.

"Our extended relatives distanced themselves," Aslam explained, "because they felt they would need to support us." At the age of 18, Aslam's father returned from Saudi Arabia after two years of failed investment. "I still remember seeing him as he exited the airplane," Aslam said. "He was barefoot and completely broken. He knew he had made a big mistake. And he never recovered. My father never worked a meaningful job again."

In the meantime, Aslam had moved to the city to attend school and work. For three years, he worked at a factory. He started his shift at 6:00 a.m., took classes at night, and sometimes did not sleep until 2:00 a.m. "When I became the provider for my family," Aslam said,

"I stopped all my Muslim rituals. I saw all my friends playing cricket and having leisure time because of their family's support. But I only had time for work and school." Aslam's mother also became sick at that time with Addison's disease. Because they sometimes lacked funds for her treatment, Aslam's stress and burden increased as the teenaged sleep-deprived breadwinner of the family.

One day, Aslam saw an advertisement for a scholarship opportunity to attend a university in Denmark. Aslam applied, was accepted, and spent the next three and a half years in Europe. Besides studying, Aslam worked to send money home. When his studies ended, Aslam returned to Bangladesh before his visa expired, but his family was angry. They were desperate for money and believed Aslam had let them down by not remaining in Denmark illegally to work. His mother's health had deteriorated, and she was nearly paralyzed. Aslam said:

> I had known my mother as kind and jolly but when I came back she was weeping and broken. I found work to try to provide, but I had no direction. I had no balance in my life. I was disconnected from peace. I hung out with bad friends, occasionally smoking and drinking with them. I was not sufficient emotionally or physically to deal with the burden. I was losing my energy, losing my life. I needed peace.

Like most people searching for peace and answers in that part of Bangladesh, Aslam visited a Muslim guru. The guru challenged Aslam to be devoted to ritual prayers and his teachings. Aslam began wearing traditional Muslim clothes again and performing the five ritual prayers a day. Aslam also started visiting the graves of dead gurus on ritual holidays and praying to these gurus for guidance and blessing. After several months, however, Aslam was disenchanted by the guru's hypocrisy and stopped following him. He also stopped visiting gurus' graves. "Why am I doing this?" Aslam thought. "How can a dead person help me?"

About that time, Aslam's mother had a terrible fall and almost died. Shortly after the accident, she called Aslam into her room. Aslam had long noticed a thick book her mother kept by her bed, but he had never asked her about it. "Take this book," his mother said. "Read it and be blessed."

"What is it?" Aslam asked.

"Read it and be blessed," his mother repeated.

His mother's fall had pressed her to subtly pass on to her son a secret she had kept by her side since childhood.[1] Aslam looked over the book his mother placed in his hands. It was battered with use; the cover was gone, pages were falling out, and the paper was turning yellow. His mother never said what it was. She simply said, "Be blessed."

Months later, Aslam grabbed the book off his shelf and discovered it was an *Injil* (the New Testament). With his Islamic mindset, Aslam was shocked his mother owned such a book since the Qur'an was the only book they were supposed to believe.

"What did you give me?" he asked his mom.

"It is my book," she said. "Read it and be blessed. It talks about Isa the Messiah. You can learn a lot about him."

Aslam read the four gospels, but they made no sense to him, and they contradicted the Qur'an. "This is blasphemous," he thought. Uncomfortable with what he read, he told his mom, "This book is stupid. These people Matthew, Mark, Luke, and John tell the same stories. Why did they waste pages saying the same thing? Besides, Christians have changed and corrupted the *Injil*."

Aslam's mother laughed and smiled. "Listen," she said. "These are four books written at four times by four people. They say the same things. They tell the same story about Isa. That's why we know the stories are true."

Since his mother, whom he loved deeply, told him the book was true, Aslam had the confidence to pick up the *Injil* again, believing there might be some answers for him inside. But as he read, he realized he did not even know the contents of the Qur'an. Even though he had spent a decade of his childhood reciting the Qur'an, he had done so in Arabic, not knowing what he was saying. Consequently, he picked up a copy of the Qur'an in his language, Bangla, and began to read. But the Qur'an was not in chronological order, and it was difficult for him to understand. "How can I know the truth?" he asked himself.

He decided to compare what the Bible and the Qur'an taught on whom he believed were the four main prophets: Abraham, Moses,

Jesus, and Mohammed. But Aslam only had a New Testament, so he began searching for a complete Bible. When Aslam asked a Catholic man at work for a Bible, the man gave him an address for his church. The people at the church questioned Aslam, discovered he was Muslim, took his phone number, and said they would call him. They never called. Aslam visited several other churches in the city in search of a Bible. Concerned about their safety, no church members met with Aslam or gave him the Book he desired.

Later that year, however, Aslam searched for someone online to give him a Bible. After many failed attempts over several months, Aslam finally connected with a pastor in Chittagong who embraced Aslam and invited him to church meetings. The pastor wrapped a Bible in cloth, showing honor for the Holy Book, and gave it to Aslam. "Read this," the pastor said, "but be cautious where you read it."

Aslam was overjoyed to receive a complete Bible, and he began his study of the prophets. Aslam said:

> As I studied, Isa popped up like daylight before me. The picture of Isa was clear. As I made my comparison, I found he was above the other prophets. God opened my eyes to see Isa's divine nature, his divine characteristics, and his divine authority. He was more than a prophet. I had difficulty believing and accepting this with my background, but it was clearly true. I felt the danger of accepting those beliefs. I was afraid. I knew shame would come upon my family and me. I thought, "Now I know the truth, so I can just let this go." And I tried to brush off my interest in the Bible.

Every time Aslam retreated from the Bible or the church to focus on his family and career, he could not stay away for long. At first, he attended church services once a month. If a church service started at 5:00 p.m., Aslam snuck in at 2:00 p.m. and did not leave until 9:00 p.m. Before and after the church meetings, Aslam asked questions and learned more about the Bible. As months passed, Aslam increased his involvement with the church.

"I discovered I was loving Jesus. I started feeling joy in my heart. But I still felt fear and confusion."

One night, Aslam had trouble sleeping. He turned on the light, picked up his Bible, and prayed. "Allah, I am so confused. Whoever you are, help me. I cannot live this life."

Aslam felt stuck. He did not accept all of Christianity, but he was no longer living as a Muslim. "I cannot stay in the middle," Aslam prayed. "Help me to know the truth. Guide me and help me."

Suddenly, Aslam felt God's presence in his life for the first time. "I felt a light upon me, a divine peace, a joy in my heart, and the comfort of a secured soul."

Aslam picked up his Bible and read John 3 and John 14 over and over again. After a while, Aslam realized something; he was Nicodemus. Nicodemus's question of, "How can these things be?"[2] expressed the same misunderstanding Aslam was having. Aslam said:

I was denying the Light that came into the world.[3] I was worried about earthly things. Shame was my main barrier. How could I leave Islam and put my family under shame? But the Scripture was clear. I needed to be born again. I needed to follow the truth and be sanctified by the blood of Jesus. But I was afraid. How could I know for sure it was worth it?

But then Aslam read Jesus's words in John 14:1-3, "Let not your hearts be troubled. Believe in God; believe also in me. In my Father's house are many rooms. If it were not so, would I have told you that I go to prepare a place for you? And if I go and prepare a place for you, I will come again and will take you to myself, that where I am you may be also."

He also read Jesus's words in John 14:6, "I am the way, and the truth, and the life. No one comes to the Father except through me."

Aslam described how he felt after reading those words:

I felt 100% assurance. I felt complete joy, and a divine peace wrapped around me. I shouted in my room with joy. For the first time in my life, I praised God from my heart in my language. I could not sleep the whole night because of my joy. I felt released from my burden, my hopelessness, and my sinful life. I felt God saying to me, "You are now part of my family. Do not worry."

The next morning, Aslam rushed to his mother and explained the joy he felt from reading Jesus's words. "She smiled at me with a divine smile," Aslam said. "Read this book and be blessed," his mother had prophesied. Her blessing and joy were silently devoured for decades from a bedside Bible. And two years before she passed away, her first child received that blessing and joy, beginning a journey with Jesus that would publicly, and dangerously, leave the same legacy to the world: "Read this book, and be blessed."

Joy and Suffering in Sharing Jesus

The first few months after Aslam felt the assurance and truth of salvation in Jesus, he intensely studied the Bible. Each day after he arrived home from work, he reached for his Bible. After those first few months, he talked to his pastor about his desire to learn more. The pastor arranged for Aslam to attend Bible conferences and seminary classes. For more than two years, Aslam grew in his faith in Christ and knowledge of the Bible, even taking time off work for Bible study classes, but his faith remained silent before Muslims. After those first couple of years, however, he began sharing with his friends and family about Isa being the Light of the World, the Spirit of God, and the path to Paradise. These friends and family began monitoring Aslam's travel and influences.

When his family discovered his association with Christians, his cousin searched his room and found Aslam's Bible. The cousin was outraged. Aslam's family and friends began mocking him and warning him that trouble would ensue if he did not change his behavior. But Aslam continued to commit his life to Jesus and shared his faith with others.

Around that time, Aslam started chatting with a college-aged girl named Fatima on the Internet. Aslam longed for a companion, but he was a follower of Christ from a Muslim background. Traditional marriages in Bangladesh required approval from both families. Muslim families would never approve of their daughter marrying a Christian. And Christian families still treated Aslam with suspicion and disapproval. Furthermore, Aslam had only met a few followers of Jesus from a Muslim background.

Nevertheless, Aslam traveled to Dhaka to meet Fatima in person. They had lunch together, enjoyed their time, and arranged to meet the next day. Fatima was from a strong Muslim family, so Aslam knew he needed to talk about his faith in Jesus before the relationship continued much longer. The next day, Aslam told Fatima, "I know you think I am a Muslim, but I must confess that I do not believe in Islam."

"What?! What do you believe?" Fatima asked.

"I believe in Isa," Aslam said.

"How dare you!" Fatima replied. "I've never heard of anyone doing this. You converted to become a Christian?!"

"Actually," Aslam said, "God is the one who converted me."

Fatima was furious. It would have been more acceptable if the person she had imagined marrying was infected with a terminal, contagious disease. She walked away from Aslam without a word.

"I thought our relationship was over," Aslam reflected, "but that night, Fatima called me and said she wanted to see me the next day."

When they saw each other, Fatima acted normally and unaffected by Aslam's beliefs, so he took her to a church. That day, Fatima made friends at church whom she continued to see after Aslam returned to Chittagong. Since Fatima lived apart from her family while at university, she felt free to attend church and make Christian friends. After a year of studying the Bible, Fatima made a confession to Aslam, "Now I know who Isa is. He is the Messiah."

"Do you think you can follow him?" Aslam asked.

"Why not?" she replied. "It is the truth!"

Fatima committed to following Christ, and later that year, Aslam and Fatima were baptized together. Fifteen months later, despite their family's disapproval, Aslam and Fatima committed their lives to the Lord as a married couple. Aslam explained:

> There's no way I should have been able to marry. Muslims wouldn't give me a wife. Christians wouldn't give me a wife. But God used me to bring Fatima to faith in Jesus, and this is how God gave me a wife. I realized at that time there is a bigger plan, that God is guiding things in his own way. It is a Superplan, actually.

And with that, a new English word was born that shows we are just actors on God's stage. God has a Superplan!

For Aslam, like many followers of Christ from Muslim backgrounds, his public display of faith in Jesus through baptism intensified disapproval and wrath from Muslim peers and family. From the time of his baptism until his arrival in America five years later, Aslam and his family were continuously slandered and mocked, and Aslam was physically attacked five times. Aslam never knew when or where the attacks would take place.

One day, he paid a visit to his cousin. "One of my brother's friends opened the door and saw me," Aslam explained. "He immediately kicked me in the chest like a karate guy with all his strength and shut the door. He knocked me back 10 feet onto the ground, and I couldn't stand up for 20 minutes as I struggled to breathe."

After the kicking incident, Aslam rushed to his church, and the pastor gave him a place to stay in the church building. Eventually, a closet was cleared out underneath a stairwell, and this room became the primary home for Aslam, and later his wife Fatima and son Fahin, for several years. Occasionally, Aslam stayed in his family's home, but doing so was risky.

"The imam ordered me to cut off your head in the middle of the night," Aslam's father confessed to him one day.

"Are you going to do it?" Aslam asked.

"No, I am not going to do it," the father replied, "but because of Islam, I should. You have to change your life and come back to Islam."

Such experiences made sleeping in his family's home difficult!

On one occasion, a cousin had Aslam tied to a chair while a mob of young men slashed at Aslam's wrists with a knife.[4] On another occasion, his uncle began beating him and did not stop until Aslam's aunts came to the rescue. A few months later, the same uncle set out to kill Aslam. As Aslam stood on a street corner outside his family's home, he saw his uncle running toward him with an angry mob of 20 men. His uncle held a butcher knife in the air, and the people yelled, "Cut off his head!"

Aslam froze. He knew he couldn't outrun the mob, so he blurted out a prayer, "Lord, help me! Lord, I need your help!"

Aslam's uncle, the same one he used to play and laugh with, was rushing at him with murder in his eyes. The butcher knife was raised, and the uncle was only a second or two from striking. Aslam stood motionless, bracing for the knife's blow. But five feet away, the uncle's eyes made contact with Aslam's; it was as if a trance lifted, restoring conscience and clarity to his uncle. He stopped abruptly. The knife fell from his hand, and he embraced Aslam.

"What happened?!" the mob cried. "Why did you stop?"

"Go away from here!" the uncle said to the mob. "Leave! And take this knife away from me! I need to talk to Aslam." Aslam's uncle was large and terrifying, so the mob left.

Aslam and his uncle sat together on the side of the road. "What's wrong, uncle?" Aslam asked.

"You should come back to Islam," his uncle replied. "I don't know why I stopped. I almost cut your head off."

"But I know why he stopped," Aslam now says with a grin.

Just because people have peace and joy in Christ does not mean they have peace with their culture in following God's Superplan. Several times, Aslam felt exhausted and isolated because of the persecution and attempted to leave God's Superplan for a quiet and safe life. He tried to keep peace with his family and society by remaining silent about Jesus, not attending church, and not reading his Bible. Aslam tried to be satisfied with the comfort that Christianity gave to himself and his family. But he found comfort and Jesus to be incompatible, so he was unable to remain silent. Aslam explained:

> It was spiritual warfare. The Spirit of God did not allow me to stay quiet. I belonged to Jesus. I was bought by his blood. I tried to rescue myself, but he was my rescuer! I thought about how my life was in a trashcan, and Jesus brought me out and cleaned me. I did not deserve his grace, but he gave it to me nonetheless. Every time I experienced persecution and trials I was nervous and scared, but when I came to my senses, I thought about Jesus on the cross and his gift of salvation. Other Christians advised me to shut my mouth and not talk about Jesus so the persecution would stop. But how could I remain silent about what Jesus did for me and what he could do for others? This is who I was—I belonged to Jesus and his Superplan.

Aslam became bolder in his witness. He read books by a Muslim apologist who tried to debunk Christianity. Aslam found out where the apologist lived, knocked on his door, and challenged his teachings. The apologist ended up warmly receiving a Bible, which he had never read. Aslam invited imams to his family's home for discussions about Jesus. He shared Christ with prominent government figures. Aslam also started traveling throughout Bangladesh to document cases of persecution against Christians.

Nearly one year after marrying Aslam, Fatima gave birth to Fahin. As Fahin became a young boy, Aslam and Fatima noticed their family and society seeking to influence Fahin by taking him to the mosque, slandering his parents' beliefs, and attempting to make him grow up as a Muslim. At that time, Aslam and Fatima prayed about moving somewhere to freely raise their child under their own influence and that of other followers of Christ. Two years later, Aslam felt that God answered his prayer by providing a way to visit America. Once in America, Aslam applied for and received asylum due to the danger of remaining in Bangladesh. Fatima and Fahin joined him the following year.

Boldness in Freedom

By coming to America, Aslam and Fatima had every opportunity to slip into a quiet life instead of staying with God's Superplan. But within a month after moving to New York City, Aslam met Brad and joined him in sharing the gospel with Bangladeshis. Aslam told Brad, "I have to do whatever I can to reach my people." Freedom in America could have meant isolation and comfort for Aslam. Instead, he found American freedom allowed him to be even more bold in sharing Christ than he had been in Bangladesh.

"My people are hungry for the truth," Aslam said, "but society's pressure binds people from investigating the life and teachings of Jesus. In America, the pressure is less. There is freedom. I see so much opportunity in America for my people to know and follow Jesus."

Aslam has found his people's minority status in America has diminished their aggression toward those with different beliefs. Even his own extended family members living in America have been more receptive to the message of Jesus.

"In Bangladesh," Aslam explained, "I was usually not given a chance to say what I believe. They persecuted me only knowing I made a decision to follow Jesus. In America, I have been able to explain to every family member why I made that decision, and they have listened to me share the gospel."

Aslam has seen other Bangladeshi Muslims in New York profess faith in Jesus and move forward with baptism and discipleship. Some of these new converts share their joy with other Muslims and have led others to salvation in Jesus. Aslam also chats on social media with Bangladeshi Muslims throughout the world with over 20,000 people following the online dialogue. This global conversation has resulted in more Muslims, even some imams, giving their lives to Jesus. Aslam could not have imagined such ministries and opportunities; they could only have come through the suffering and joy of sharing Jesus in the Superplan of God.

God's Superplan
Aslam's life epitomizes the same journey I have been seeking to live ever since God challenged me in a Texas parking lot to do what he wanted instead of merely inviting him into *my* life—*my* preferences, *my* conditions, and *my* limitations. What if we simply gave our lives to Jesus and his Superplan and let him work out the details in how all our suffering and successes worked together for his glory?

Finding and equipping people like Aslam became a new role God had for me in his Superplan, and my efforts began spreading beyond West Africans to other unreached people groups. This new role was out of my comfort zone, not in my experience, and not my preference. The role was also risky and faced more opposition than I could have imagined. But as Aslam so poignantly articulated and exemplifies, discomfort, contention, and uncertainty are normal—in God's Superplan.

---

[1] Aslam suspects his mother received the book decades beforehand while attending a middle school which had several church buildings nearby.

[2] "Do not marvel that I said to you, 'You must be born again.' The wind blows where it wishes, and you hear its sound, but you do not know where it comes from or where it goes. So it is with everyone who is born of the Spirit." Nicodemus said to him, "How can these things be?" Jesus answered him, "Are you the teacher of Israel and yet you do not understand these things?" (John 3:7-9).

[3] "Whoever believes in him is not condemned, but whoever does not believe is condemned already, because he has not believed in the name of the only Son of God. And this is the judgment: the light has come into the world, and people loved the darkness rather than the light because their works were evil" (John 3:18-19).

[4] Aslam has around eight scars across his wrist today from the incident. Aslam's screams were so loud that the mob abruptly left in fear of being discovered.

But he said to me, "My grace is sufficient for you, for my power is made perfect in weakness." Therefore I will boast all the more gladly of my weaknesses, so that the power of Christ may rest upon me. For the sake of Christ, then, I am content with weaknesses, insults, hardships, persecutions, and calamities. For when I am weak, then I am strong (2 Corinthians 12:9-10).

SOMETIMES GOD'S SUPERPLAN REQUIRES us to alter our relationships with good people and organizations. When God desires us to leave the status quo, these changes invite conflict.

In the late 18th century, when William Carey was a newly ordained minister without a college education, he challenged his superiors about the church's lack of involvement in spreading the gospel to the world. An elder minister jumped to his feet and cried out in response, "Young man, sit down; when God pleases to convert the heathen world, he will do it without your help or mine."[1]

William Carey sat down momentarily, but then rose up again to transcend the limited paradigm of his colleagues, delivering a powerful sermon and essay in 1792 that launched the modern missions movement.[2] Carey's life and work in India embodied the sermon's message: "Expect great things from God. Attempt great things for God."[3]

When I prayed and asked God what it would take to see the unreached peoples of Metro New York reached, he challenged me to expect and attempt greater things. God's people had access to more unreached people groups in our city than perhaps anywhere else in the world, but we were doing little among them. Something had to change.

Providing Answers

Even before I began asking the "what's it going to take?" question, God was already providing answers. One of those answers came through Brad, his wife Sara, and their children, who had recently moved to the city. Brad's family had spent almost a decade working among Muslims in Southeast Asia. Like Nichole and me, they had envisioned living their entire lives overseas working among Muslims. Through a variety of circumstances that seemed at the time like great detours and disappointments, God had led them back to the States to join in his Superplan.

Brad and Sara's family spent a year in South Carolina wrestling with God about what to do and where to live. "It was a dark time," Brad confessed. "We still had a burden to share Jesus with Muslims, but God had clearly called us to return. We struggled with how to continue our calling, but God kept reminding us that our primary calling was to obey him, not to fulfill our ideas about life and missions."

Someone suggested that Brad and Sara move to New York City, where one million Muslims reside. Upon visiting Muslim enclaves in the city, God broke their heart for the people, and they moved to Queens three weeks later. Brad started working as a real estate agent to support his family, and he and Sara began sharing the gospel with Muslims.

Hundreds of thousands of South Asian Muslims lived in the city compared to a much smaller population of Southeast Asian Muslims, so Brad and Sara shifted focus to work with Bangladeshis and Pakistanis. "If God initiated movements of Muslims to Christ elsewhere in the world," Brad stated, "he could do the same in New York City." With that confidence in the Lord, Brad and Sara began devoting themselves to their new vision.

Brad and I discussed what needed to take place. We needed to see an increase in workers among unreached peoples. And to see that happen, a new dedicated organization was needed, one that would mobilize and sustain effective missionaries among the unreached in a globalized world of transnational relationships. Without each other, I do not think Brad or I would have entertained such an idea.

We wrote down the pros and cons of establishing a new organization. The con list was four times longer. I didn't want to start an organization; neither did Brad and Sara. We were too busy already, and we knew we'd need to fulfill roles that would pull us away from the ministry we loved. I didn't like administrative roles or organizational management. I became bored at board meetings. Among my teammates in Africa, my disdain for working on logistics, handling money, and doing administrative tasks became a running joke. I wanted to be with people! Being responsible for establishing and managing an organization was not my desire or my gifting.

But God's Superplan is not about our preferences. His Superplan is not even about our experiences or gifting. I have filled out a variety of "spiritual gift inventories" in the past. The purpose of these inventories is to help people discover their spiritual gifts by answering questions about preferences, inclinations, and habits. Such inventories are valuable for helping people discover their natural gifts, but the inventories are destructive when they lead people to believe that God can only use their strengths.[4]

No gift is more spiritual than God giving people abilities they do not possess naturally. God led the slow-of-speech and ineloquent Moses to free the Israelites (Exodus 4:10-11). God made a prophet out of Amos who was neither a prophet nor the son of a prophet, but a shepherd and a caretaker of fruit trees (Amos 7:14). God used ordinary and uneducated men like Peter and John to build his church (Acts 4:13). The list could go on. When we live for God's Superplan, we don't allow what we perceive to be our spiritual gifts to dictate our decisions. God often uses a person's weakness to do incredible acts that point more to his glory and grace than to the person's ability.

Despite our preferences, we were compelled to move forward in starting an organization called Global Gates.[5] The name came from gateways the Lord provided in recent times to access a large variety of the world's least-reached peoples, and unreached places, through cities. When Paul addressed the people of Athens, he said, "[God] made from one man every nation of mankind to live on all the face of the earth, having determined allotted periods and the boundaries of their dwelling place, that they should seek God" (Acts

17:26-27). The Bible says God is behind the moving and location of the world's peoples for a specific reason—that they should seek him!

In starting a mission organization that focuses on immigrants with little or no Christian presence, we faced opposition. Nothing that is born comes out easy! Each time we were close to finalizing Global Gates as an organization, unexpected obstacles arose. I heard,

"You can't do this."

"What you're doing hasn't been done so we can't support you."

"You're going to step on toes."

"You'll be competing with us for funds."

Even though I was certain a new organization was needed to increase mission outreach to unreached peoples, my efforts invited conflict with people and organizations I respected. And I don't like upsetting people!

I spent long nights trying to release anxiety to the Lord and racing with thoughts on how to overcome a litany of obstacles. At one point, I was told by mentors to bury Global Gates and dig it up a few years later. They saw the difficulties we were up against and did not see a way out.

My mentors were concerned for me personally. They knew starting an organization, instead of simply doing whatever fit into the culture of existing Christian organizations, was risky financially, professionally, and relationally. I was confronted with a difficult choice. I could back down from starting Global Gates, which most people deemed the responsible choice, or I could push forward with starting an organization to increase workers among unreached people groups. These are the Superplan choices of life. Both options were permissible, but what would the Lord desire if we did not allow risk, relational pressure, and financial insecurity to cloud our decision?

After many days of prayer and counsel, we launched Global Gates. Before I left the security, partnerships, and credibility of working with an established organization, I was hiking in a park when I came across a spider. God usually speaks to me in conventional ways through prayer, his Word, and the Church, but on this occasion, he also spoke through a dangling spider that my face came within inches of hitting. I didn't see the spider because it had no web; it seemed suspended in mid-air. Upon closer inspection, I noticed a single strand of silk connecting the spider to a tree branch several yards above. The spider swung freely with the wind, uninhibited by a web or other structure. It seemed without support, but it was secure and free. I felt the Lord saying something similar to me. Even though I would leave behind a web of safety for the unknown, the Lord was my security, and freedom was found in following his voice instead of the reasoning of man's.

The Ends of the Earth Have Moved

The establishment of Global Gates marked a distinct transition in our lives and ministry. I had operated with the mission of "being the one Christian someone knows" for most of my adult life. After founding Global Gates, however, I spent most of my time interviewing and training new missionaries, building organizational structures and procedures, and helping solve conflicts and problems. In the past, when people would ask our small children what their father did for work, they would say, "He visits African friends and tells them about Jesus." Over time, even though I still visited African friends and told them about Jesus, our youngest children began answering, "He works on the computer." Their answers were jarring to me, but my kids noticed the obvious transition.

"Unless a grain of wheat falls into the earth and dies," Jesus said, "it remains alone; but if it dies, it bears much fruit" (John 12:24).

Starting Global Gates meant dying to my extensive ministry involvement on the frontlines so more fruit could be born through others. Brad and Sara experienced a similar death. In God's Superplan, we don't make choices based on personal fulfillment but obedience to God. Our obedience and love for God, in turn, make the new directions from the Lord joyful and fulfilling.

I discovered joy in "living for the success of others" through developing the ministries of Global Gates. My calling evolved from being the one Christian someone knows to mobilizing and training others to reach unreached peoples in accessible cities so they could be the one Christian someone knows, and communities of Christ-followers could disseminate around the world. Sometimes God's

Superplan requires aspects of our life and ministry to fall to the ground and die so a more fruitful harvest can arise.

That grain of wheat began falling the moment Brad and I asked the question, "What is it going to take to reach the unreached people groups across New York City?" Most of us who live for God's Superplan focus at first on our activity, building skills useful in sharing the gospel, and joining God's work where our natural interests align.

Because most of us are unskilled at sharing the gospel cross-culturally, it is natural to focus at first on learning language and culture, and how to effectively communicate the gospel with people who have different worldviews. Over time, however, workers in God's Superplan need to become even more "others-centric" in their thinking and activity. The question shifts from, "What can I do?" to, "How can the gospel message be best understood and received by the people I am sharing with?" and, "How can this work be reproduced beyond me?" Simply being the one Christian someone knows doesn't address those two larger questions.

Through the founding of Global Gates, I have seen multiplying fruit in answer to all those questions. All types of people have joined God's Superplan as the Lord has "sent out laborers into his harvest" (Luke 10:2).[6]

Since we established Global Gates, we have seen Christians from across the country leave successful careers to invest their lives among immigrants in cities with Global Gates. Students have left promising career paths; church staff members have left their comfortable parishes; bankers and accountants have joined the growing movement. They have sold (or given away) homes, vehicles, and other possessions to be Christ's presence among people who have no idea what these new missionaries left behind.

A man from Mexico came to faith in Christ in the Bronx and utilized his workplace for befriending and sharing the gospel with West African Muslims. I discovered him through a Muslim friend who called me and said, "You have to meet this guy. He is like you. He can help distribute God's Word to our people!" This Mexican man did not let his broken English or long hours at work deter him from playing a role in God's Superplan.

A Muslim woman from West Africa migrated to Europe where she came to faith in Christ. Decades into her successful career, God called her to move from France to become a missionary in New York City. Although the instruction she received from God was limited, she left her career and began ministering to homeless people and drug addicts in a city where she knew no one. After several years, God gave her the desire to join our ministry through Global Gates. As one of the few Christians among her staunchly Muslim ethnic group, God has opened doors for her to share the gospel with her people in ways she had never dreamed possible.

Within weeks of coming to Christ in Harlem, a West African woman shared Jesus with imams and sorcerers. She has not only led others to faith in Christ in New York City, but has also traveled to her home country and led family members to Jesus, all within the first few months of becoming a believer. One of the women she led to Christ in the city has seen Jesus bring reconciliation to her fractured family in West Africa. Her Muslim father now testifies that Jesus united his family! The gospel is naturally crossing the ocean from diaspora populations in Western gateway cities and transforming lives in Africa, Asia, and elsewhere.

A local pastor once told me, "Global Gates is an idea whose time has come." For years we have been sending our very best to the ends of the earth; now the ends of the earth are sending their very best to us. Because the world is moving to cities,[7] the next challenge for missionary pioneers is not just reaching people in remote villages, but reaching busy, hidden, influential unreached peoples who have migrated to global gateway cities.[8]

Even the people of Bandogo, who have no electricity or running water, now have cell phones that connect them to big daddies and big mommas in cities. When I lived as a missionary in a middle-class neighborhood in Bamako, I never met a homeowner because they lived behind walled compounds or in other countries. In New York City, however, I have met up to 10 people who owned homes in that same Bamako neighborhood. I had more access to these homeowners—and thus the entire household—by living in New York City rather than in their neighborhood in Africa!

Jesus said, "You will be my witnesses in Jerusalem and in all Judea and Samaria, and to the end of the earth" (Acts 1:8). Right out of college, I moved to the end of the earth in Mali. But I didn't realize the Lord was moving the ends of the earth to Manhattan and elsewhere. My family couldn't return to Africa because of my broken health, but the Lord used my sickness so we could stumble into one of the most strategic frontiers of missions. What Satan intended for evil, God has used for good (Genesis 50:20).

Within the global gateway cities[9] where missionaries from Global Gates serve, places such as New York City, Houston, and Toronto, the large concentrations and varieties of unreached people groups create open doors for the gospel to jump from culture to culture, multiplying and bouncing from the city to places around the world with little Christian witness.

The people in these cities have daily contact, in some ways, with most places on the planet. As the message of hope in Jesus becomes part of these daily contacts and conversations, we will witness an unprecedented natural flow of the gospel message throughout the world. Beyond what we know, the gospel is already riding the waves of globalization and transnationalism, disseminating from these cities into areas and peoples long untouched by its transformative power.

Global Gates, for the glory of God, exists for that purpose.

---

[1] Joseph Belcher, *William Carey: A Biography* (Philadelphia: American Baptist Publication Society, 1853), 19.

[2] William Carey, *An Enquiry into the Obligations of Christians to Use Means for the Conversion of the Heathens* (Leicester, England: Ann Ireland, 1792).

[3] S Pearce Carey, *William Carey* (London: The Wakeman Trust, 1923), 77.

[4] These inventories may also identify strengths that have only developed since a person became a Christ-follower.

[5] You can find more information about Global Gates' vision of reaching the ends of the earth through global gateway cities at www.globalgates.info.

[6] "And [Jesus] said to them, 'The harvest is plentiful, but the laborers are few. Therefore pray earnestly to the Lord of the harvest to send out laborers into his harvest'" (Luke 10:2). On most days over the last few years, an alarm has sounded on my phone at 10:02 a.m. as a reminder to pray for laborers as Jesus instructed.

[7] At the beginning of the 20th century, only 13% of the world's population lived in urban areas. According to a 2014 United Nations report, today 54% of the world's population reside in cities, and that percentage is expected to rise to 66% by 2050. United Nations, *World Urbanization Prospects: 2014 Revision* (New York: United Nations, 2014), esa.un.org/unpd/wup/Publications/Files/WUP2014-Highlights.pdf, Accessed 14 Oct. 2016.

[8] For further research, see Jared Looney, *Crossroads of the Nations: Diaspora, Globalization, and Evangelism* (Skyforest, CA: Urban Loft Publishers, 2015); Sadiri Joy Tira and Tetsunao Yamamori, editors, *Scattered and Gathered: A Global Compendium of Diaspora Missiology* (Eugene, OR: Wipf and Stock Publishers, 2016); J.D. Payne, *Strangers Next Door: Immigration, Migration and Mission* (Westmont, IL: IVP Books, 2012); Paul G. Hiebert, "Missionary as Mediator of Global Theologizing," *Paul G. Hiebert Global Center for Intercultural Studies*, n.d., hiebertglobalcenter.org/blog/wp-content/uploads/2013/03/Hiebert-Article-1-Missionary-as-Mediator-of-Global-Theologizing.pdf, Accessed 9 Apr. 2017; and Chris Clayman, "Reaching the Nations Through Our Cities," *Great Commission Research Journal*, vol. 6, no. 1, 2014, pp. 6-21.

[9] To see how Global Gates defines a "global gateway city" for Kingdom purposes, visit "Defining Global Gateway Cities," *Global Gates*, n.d., www.globalgates.info/what-are-global-gateway-cities/, Accessed 27 Oct. 2016.

Conclusion

But thanks be to God, who in Christ always leads us in triumphal procession, and through us spreads the fragrance of the knowledge of him everywhere. For we are the aroma of Christ to God among those who are being saved and among those who are perishing, to one a fragrance from death to death, to the other a fragrance from life to life (2 Corinthians 2:14-16).

IN CHAPTER EIGHT OF the Book of Acts, there is an unusual story of God spreading his message of salvation through a servant of the church named Philip. After one of his colleagues named Stephen had been martyred, Philip traveled to Samaria to proclaim the message of Jesus to the Samaritans. Up until that point in the early history of the church, followers of Jesus were almost exclusively mainstream Jews. The Jews viewed Samaritans as half-breed unclean neighbors to be despised and avoided. But Jesus told his disciples to be his witnesses not only in Jerusalem and Judea (to the Jews), but also in Samaria and the ends of the earth (even to the enemies of the Jews).

Philip was the first person in the Book of Acts to be a witness to his culture's enemy. In Samaria, large crowds of Samaritans were healed in Jesus's name and responded with joy to the gospel. Many were baptized and received the Holy Spirit. Philip was being used in the most dynamic activity of God anywhere in the world. He was a pioneer missionary seeing spiritual breakthroughs that unveiled a new era of God's redemptive plan. With such a large response to the gospel message, Philip could have been busy for years discipling new believers and establishing churches. Where else would he desire to go?

But then, God spoke to Philip through an angel with the following instructions: "Rise and go toward the south to the road that goes down from Jerusalem to Gaza. This is a desert place" (Acts 8:26).

There were a couple of routes connecting Jerusalem to Gaza. The route Philip was instructed to take through the desert was less traveled.[1] I can only imagine what Philip felt and heard as he listened to the Lord's command:

Get up Philip. Go on the road from Jerusalem to Gaza. Don't take the populated routes; take the one through the desert. I can't give you any more instructions than that. Yes, I know there are many needs around you. Yes, I know you feel your current activity is important and purposeful. Yes, I know you are seeing me do things never seen before. But I want you to go to a deserted road. Okay?

What?! The instructions were absurd!

But Philip was invested in the Superplan of God, because his response to God was immediate. "He rose and went" (Acts 8:27). Simple obedience. No questions of: "Why would I do that when there is so much going on here? Why the desert road? What exactly will I be doing? Will it offer the same opportunities or be as strategic as what I am doing in Samaria?" No statements of delayed obedience: "Okay, I'll go, but there are a few important tasks to take care of here first." Philip heard the call of the Lord, obeyed, and took the next step of faith into the unknown of God's Superplan.

Because Philip was immersed in a plan bigger than his own, he left for the desert road. Because he left for the desert road, the Lord revealed to him the next step on the adventure. "Go over and get close to that chariot that's coming."

Philip didn't know what awaited him. He was simply told to approach the chariot. Once again, the Lord gave the next step of instruction without explaining what would happen.

Because Philip obeyed and took the desert road, and because he obeyed and approached the chariot, he was only then able to see God's activity and the specifics on how to be involved. An Ethiopian eunuch was in the chariot who was the head treasurer of Ethiopia. And he was returning home with the Word of God in his hands after worshipping in Jerusalem. How and why the eunuch was worshipping in Jerusalem and reading the Word of God, we do not know.

But he was reading a messianic passage from the Old Testament book of Isaiah.

"Do you understand what you are reading?" Philip asked (Acts 8:31).

"How can I," the eunuch replied, "unless someone guides me?" (Acts 8:31).

Philip explained how the passage prophesied about Jesus and shared the good news of what Jesus had done to bring salvation to those who believe. Farther down the road, the eunuch said, "See, here is water! What prevents me from being baptized?" (Acts 8:37). He was baptized, and he went on his way rejoicing.

Philip could have stayed in Samaria, quietly disobeyed God, and everyone would still have viewed him as an exemplary Christian. But because Philip was obedient to leave success and follow God into the unknown, God used him in a second groundbreaking event. Philip had a fruitful ministry among the Samaritans; why leave? Only he would have known his heart's disobedience. But as it turned out, Philip was able to be part of something far bigger than himself: the gospel of Jesus spreading to Africa for the first time.

How many of us miss out on fantastic adventures with God because of our disobedience or delayed willingness to obey? How often do we miss out on the joy of being used by God because we want more specifics on what we will be doing or the chances of success? Do we lack specific direction from God because we have never developed a general obedience and passion for God and his passions?

If we knew too much about what the future held, perhaps we would be too fearful, anxious, or cautious to move forward. Perhaps we would view God's ways of accomplishing his purposes as too strange, causing us to question if we were genuinely hearing the voice of the Lord. Think of Philip's situation. A eunuch was a castrated man. A gender-altered male is the one God chose to bring the gospel to Africa through Philip. Would Philip have taken that journey if he had known who God was going to use? Would you or I? God's Superplan is full of surprises.

Becoming an Actor on God's Stage

"What more shall I say? For time would fail me to tell of..."[2] So begins a verse from Hebrews that describes the faith of people God has used throughout his Story. I could tell the same of ordinary people today living extraordinary lives within God's Superplan: Christians with little money in the bank giving their car to someone in need, servants of Christ housing Saudi Muslim students, disciples used by God in their workplace to love their co-workers as God loves them. But no matter how many stories told and examples given of how God has led me and other individuals, God doesn't want copies of other people.

You are unique, and your story within God's Superplan will be unique. I hope the stories in this book have inspired you, but you can't be transformed by our stories. You can only be transformed by assuming your unique role as an actor on God's stage.

Some of us might be tempted to discouragement because of the dissonance we experience between our lives and the stories of people highly invested in God's Superplan. We must remember, however, that following God's Superplan is a process. We can't let someone else's faith journey paralyze us from making steps in the right direction.

The process of joining God's Superplan begins with acknowledging the existence of the Superplan and asking God to use us in his Story. That moment for me took place in a Texas parking lot when I switched questions from, "What am I supposed to do (as informed by the culture, including Christian culture, around me)?" to, "What does God want me to do (even when his desires were counter-cultural)?"

"All the world's a stage," Shakespeare observed, "and all the men and women merely players."[3] John Calvin commented on a Psalm, "The whole world is a theater for the display of the divine goodness, wisdom, justice, and power, but the Church is the orchestra, as it were—the most conspicuous part of it."[4] Beforehand, I invited God to be an Actor in my play. Now, I am a player in God's Story.

Many of us treat Christianity as a set of cognitive truths, a ticket to heaven, or as guidance for improved moral behavior. But God gives us the relational opportunity to live for more than these religious tenets. God calls us to be his disciples with lives more dynamic than we might otherwise allow. Disciples are people who love Christ, follow him, obey him, share him with others, allow him to transform their worldview, and train others to do the same.[5] Disciples re-orient their lives to the great adventure of God redeeming all peoples to himself.

One way to discover if we are living for God's Superplan is to examine how we make decisions. Are the decisive factors for what we do and where we live our security and comfort? Personal preferences and desires? Expectations of others and the cultural gravity around us? Is the primary factor in our decision-making anything other than the glory God will receive by obeying him?

The Bible says, "Through us [God] spreads the fragrance of the knowledge of him everywhere. For we are the aroma of Christ to God among those who are being saved and among those who are perishing, to one a fragrance from death to death, to the other a fragrance from life to life" (2 Corinthians 2:14-16).

Take the smell test for yourself. When our identity is found in Jesus and our lives are devoted to his Superplan, we carry the aroma of Christ. To those God is drawing to himself, that smell is life. To those who refuse to live with Jesus as their Savior and Guide, that smell is death. If Christ's smell on us is not enough to evoke occasional repulsion or attraction from people, we should examine our role in God's Superplan. Do we smell like the culture around us or the fragrant aroma of Christ?

Actors on God's stage do not pursue suffering. But when we lay down our lives and surrender our course to the winding river of God's guidance, we come to embrace suffering and challenges, knowing they fit into a larger story in ways we might not ever know.

Although Musa, Yusuf, and Aslam never desired persecution, and I never desired physical illness, those trials were so clearly a part of God's plans and the shaping of our character that we would not change them. Our suffering sometimes brings us to the brink of abandoning the Superplan, but God's grace sustains us. As a result of this journey, we come to know God more deeply than we did before. That reality is the paradoxical nature of God's Superplan. Those who endure the greatest suffering and trials while clinging to their role in God's Superplan often experience the greatest joy and purpose in the Body of Christ.

What would the world look like if we all lived for his Superplan? What if the fragrant aroma of Christ permeated our calendars, bank accounts, credit cards statements, and relationships?

We are all just actors.

Are we lost in our own stories?

Or found in God's Superplan?

---

[1] Simon J. Kistemaker, *New Testament Commentary: Acts* (Grand Rapids: Baker, 1990) 311.

[2] Hebrews 11:32.

[3] William Shakespeare, *As You Like It*, Act II, Scene vii, Jaques to Duke Senior.

[4] John Calvin, *Commentary on the Book of Psalms, vol. 5* (Calvin Translation Society, 1849) 178.

[5] See Appendix 2 "What is a Disciple?"

appendix 1
Ideas for Entering God's Superplan

I HOPE YOU HAVE been inspired by this book to live for God's Superplan. But your inspiration will not lead to activity if you do not take practical next steps. I cannot determine what those steps should be for you, but I provide suggestions below under different categories that fit into God's Superplan. For a more extensive list of "next step" ideas, visit Superplan's website: www.theSuperplan. com

Pray

1. Create a name list. Write down everyone you know who is not walking with Christ. Include family members and friends, work colleagues or schoolmates, and those who have common hobbies or interests with you. Ask God to point out five individuals on your list. Pray intentionally for these five people and seek opportunities to share your testimony and the gospel message with them.

2. Regularly pray for and encourage missionaries you know.

3. In your home, small group, or church, adopt an unreached people group around the world or in your city and begin strategically praying for this group.

Learn

1. Learn which people groups are still unreached by visiting www. joshuaproject.net or www.peoplegroups.org.

2. Learn about unreached people groups in your city through literature and the diaspora people group databases www.peoplegroups.info (North America) and www.peoplegroups.eu (Europe).

3. Ask open-ended questions to immigrants in your city or region to learn about their culture and religion.

Go

1. Start sharing the gospel with people.

2. Start intentionally shopping and eating in places that put you in contact with members of unreached people groups. (Yes, you can buy rice from a supermarket and use self-checkout to avoid talking to anyone, but you can also buy rice at the local Muslim grocery store. Which option gives you more Superplan opportunities?!).

3. Visit the families of immigrant friends you have made from unreached people groups in their home countries and their connected diaspora communities around the world.

4. Visit www.GlobalGates.info or another mission agency's website to explore joining them "on mission" on a short-term, mid-term, or long-term basis.

Mobilize

1. Host seminars or trainings in your church about missions, evangelism with different religious groups, and spreading God's vision for reaching the nations.

2. Invite local or returning missionaries to speak in your church.

3. Encourage someone you know to consider long-term cross-cultural missionary service.

Welcome

1. Teach English with an existing organization to form natural relationships with members of unreached people groups.

2. Invite contacts or friends from unreached people groups to your home for tea or coffee.

3. Invite yourself over to homes of people from unreached people groups for tea or coffee (Westerners feel like they are imposing, but most members of unreached people groups feel honored when people express a desire to visit their homes).

Send

1. Ask a ministry or missionary among unreached people groups how you can best assist the work. Sometimes the help most needed involves skills you practice in your day job (administrative, legal, graphic and web design, marketing, etc.).

2. Financially support missionaries through contacts from your local church or personal network, or through contacting Global Gates or another missionary sending agency.

appendix 2
What is a disciple?

IN THE BOOK'S CONCLUSION, I gave the following definition: *Disciples are people who love Christ, follow him, obey him, share him with others, allow him to transform their worldview, and train others to do the same.* Discipleship is too often characterized as the accumulation of knowledge and understanding of doctrine. "Come to our discipleship program" means come to a classroom with a student workbook for lecture-style teaching. One can obtain knowledge and understand doctrine, however, without ever being a disciple of Jesus. Knowledge and doctrine are important, but only as far as they are obeyed.

There are more theologically astute and mature followers of Christ than I am who will emphasize other characteristics of disciples in a definition, and they might have solid reasons for doing so. Nevertheless, I make an attempt at defining a disciple to better understand what a disciple is and does in the New Testament pattern of following Jesus. Jesus instructed us to "make disciples," yet somehow along the way, people's salvation and baptism experiences have become our primary focus without adequate attention to what happens to them afterward. Granted, initial expressions of faith in Christ and baptisms are important and easier to quantify and measure, but the longer and more involved concept of making disciples should not dissuade us from its importance. Since Jesus emphasized making disciples, should we not have the same emphasis? I am still learning how to be a disciple and make disciples. Sometimes I feel like more of a disciple than at other times, but I pass on to you what I am learning.

In my definition, I focus on the activity of being a disciple in relationship with Christ. The attempt is to draw attention to our "relating to" instead of "knowing about." Therefore, as in any relationship, the act of being a disciple is an ongoing process that can be nurtured, deepened, and matured through time. It also means that no one arrives at a level when the activities of a disciple cease. None of us have fully arrived. Below, I unpack the definition further. May the Lord help us grow and mature as disciples of Christ who make disciples!

Disciples Are People Who:

Love Christ – Loving Christ, and accepting Christ's love, are at the core of disciples' lives and identities. We can have knowledge, ministry gifts, and even extraordinary faith, but if we do not have love, we are nothing (1 Corinthians 13:1-3). If we love anything, or anyone, more than Jesus, we are not worthy of him (Matthew 10:37, Mark 10:17-27). Jesus said the greatest commandments are to love God and love our neighbors (Matthew 22:24-40). People will know we are disciples if we love one another (John 13:35), and what we have done to the least of our neighbors we have done to him (Matthew 25:42-45).

Follow Him – Disciples are apprentices and followers of someone. Their identities and purposes are marked by their close relationship with the one they follow. Disciples of Jesus, therefore, are people who follow him and learn from him, so that his way and life become their own. Jesus's first disciples answered his invitation: "Follow me" (Luke 5:27). Jesus also told his disciples, "If anyone would come after me, let him deny himself and take up his cross and *follow me*" (Matthew 16:24, italics mine).

Obey Him – Jesus said that if we love him, we will obey his commands (John 14:15,21). Disciples are to be doers of God's Word and not hearers only (James 1:22). People cannot obey, however, what they do not know to obey. Therefore, growing in knowledge and understanding of the truth of God's Word is essential to obedience.

Share Him with Others – When disciples love, follow, and obey Jesus, they share him with others. Being a disciple is not a self-focused endeavor. It is about reflecting God's glory in and to the world, which means we must share the good news of Jesus. Jesus told his disciples, "Let your light shine before others, so that they may see your good works and give glory to your Father who is in heaven" (Matthew 5:16). He also told his disciples, "Follow me, and I will make you become fishers of men" (Mark 1:17).

Allow Him to Transform Their Worldview – All people have particular ways they view the world that are formed at an early age. Worldviews are difficult to acknowledge and change, which means Christians throughout the world have aspects of their worldviews that are more cultural than biblical. Sometimes cultural beliefs and norms are in opposition to God's Word, but Christians within those cultures may have trouble seeing or changing that aspect of their worldview. Whether Christians' worldviews are affected by the general culture or family dynamics (e.g., a father's treatment of a child can affect the child's view of God), the process of allowing the gospel of Jesus to transform people's deep-rooted worldviews lasts a lifetime. Disciples are not to conform to the world but are to be transformed by the renewal of their mind (Romans 12:2). A disciple is a new creature in Christ, throwing away the old self to put on the new self in God's likeness (2 Corinthians 5:17, Ephesians 4:22-24).

Train Others to Do the Same – One of Christ's last commands to his disciples was to make more disciples (Matthew 28:19). To be a disciple is to make disciples. Paul told Timothy, "What you have heard from me in the presence of many witnesses entrust to faithful men, who will be able to teach others also" (2 Timothy 2:2). In that one passage, four generations of disciples are present— Paul, Timothy, faithful men, and others. Disciples make disciples that make disciples. The word "train" is deliberately chosen over "teach." Making disciples entails more than teaching knowledge to someone else. Making disciples involves training others, which involves teaching, but also includes modeling and leading apprentices in a way of life. As disciples, we need to take on apprentices to tell, and show, what we know. Paul said, "Be imitators of me, as I am of Christ" (1 Corinthians 11:1).

acknowledgments

THIS BOOK WOULD NOT have been possible without my wife, Nichole, and three children (*"May God make our campfire last a long time"*). More people than I can name have contributed to my family's life, and as a result, this book. Thank you all! Special thanks to Tom, Sharon, David, Joe, Debbie, and Drew, who all contributed invaluable feedback and edits on early drafts of this book. Also, thanks to Nichole, David, mom, dad, Brittni, Valerie, Kris, Julie, and AnnMarie for your last-minute feedback on edits. You all have humbled me with your time, skill, and encouragement. I pray the Lord brings much fruit from your labor!

about the author

CHRIS CLAYMAN IS THE Co-Founder of Global Gates (www.globalgates.info), a mission organization focused on reaching the ends of the earth through global gateway cities. He has been involved in pioneer church planting in urban and rural West Africa and New York City among unreached Muslim peoples. Chris is also the author of *ethNYcity: The Nations, Tongues, and Faiths of Metropolitan New York* (unreachednewyork.com). Chris lives with his wife Nichole and three children in New York City.